Northrop Frye

NEW WORLD PERSPECTIVES

General Editors   *Arthur and Marilouise Kroker*

AVAILABLE

TECHNOLOGY AND THE CANADIAN MIND: INNIS/McLUHAN/
GRANT
Arthur Kroker

NORTHROP FRYE: A VISION OF THE NEW WORLD
David Cook

CULTURE CRITIQUE: FERNAND DUMONT AND NEW QUEBEC
SOCIOLOGY
Michael A. Weinstein

NORTHROP FRYE

A Vision of the New World

David Cook

New World Perspectives
Montréal

New World Perspective/Perspectives Nouveau Monde
7141 Sherbrooke, O.
Montréal, Québec
H4B 1M8

Distributed in Canada by: Oxford University Press
                           70 Wynford Drive
                           Don Mills, Ontario   M3C 1J9

Canadian Cataloguing in Publication Data

Cook, David Bruce, 1946-
   Northrop Frye

(New World Perspectives)
Bibliography: p.
ISBN 0-920393-12-8 (bound).
ISBN 0-920393-10-1 (pbk.)

1. Frye, Northrop, 1912 – Criticism and interpretation
2. Frye, Northrop, 1912 – Political and social views.

I. Title   II. Series

PN75.F7C65 1985   801'.95'0924   C85-090166-9

Printed and bound in Canada

CONTENTS

Preface

Preface

In the beginning . . .

In the beginning the Americans created America, and America is the beginning of the world.

Divisions on a Ground[1]

The image that informs the study is closer to that of the caricature than that of the photograph. There is no attempt to recreate Northrop Frye with the verisimilitude of the photocopying machine. Frye's works themselves are easily accessible for those with that end in mind. Thus, the study claims to be neither definitive nor complete. It presents a Frye whose features have been pulled and twisted: not a Frye who is represented. I join the artist in this task. Following Frye's own thoughts, this study is itself an order of words, subject to the same powers of the imagination as other works, however short of the mark it might be. Hence, it is both fictional and nonfictional.

The perspective adopted in this study is not traditional in another respect in that it does not deal with Frye's works from the vantage point of the literary critic. The concern here will be with Frye as a social critic and, in particular, with Frye's defense of liberalism and his critique of technology. The bulk of Frye's writings deals with the tradition as it is given from the great writers in Europe; yet, his response to these writers has in an important way been fashioned by his own experience in North America and, more particularly, in Canada. In Frye's mythology, as one also finds it in the mythology of William Blake, the New World symbolizes humanity's attempt at forming a new vision. Thus, the main theme of this study is Northrop Frye's "America: A Prophecy"; a vision of the New World.

William Blake, *America: A Prophecy*

1

A Larger Human Brain

A larger human brain will be developed by Man when the whole of human life is seen and understood as a single mental form. This single mental form is a drama of creation, struggle, redemption and restoration in the fallen life of a divine Man. This drama is the archetype of all prophecy and art, the universal form which art reveals in pieces, and it is also the Word of God, the end of the journey of our intellectual powers.

Fearful Symmetry[1]

The latter stages of the modern world have been characterized by the problem of communication. For those individuals who have been placed by a turn of the wheel of fortune in the New World, in the middle of "nowhere", the necessity to communicate with others has taken on a physical as well as a spiritual dimension. This, of course, has been the fate of anyone whose ark has run aground in the northern half of the New World, and more particularly, in the tundra regions that begin north of the 49th parallel. The struggle for survival, however, has given rise to a series of remarkable thinkers who have made it their business to struggle with the consequences of finding themselves within what is aptly termed "the wilderness." This immediately heightened the concern for identity. In particular, it has placed the crisis of existential identity in a physical locale where, quite literally, the world ends, and with it, one's existence in a matter of a few steps from wherever one happens to be. It also heightened the sense of the need for a community as witnessed by such an absurd task in Canada as that of linking the various outposts scattered along the Hudson's Bay Company trading route.

The effect of the landscape has displaced what has traditionally been the role of the "Giants in time" with the new spectre of the "Giants" who will conquer space. Canadian cultural discourse has been rich in such attempts — witness the lines of communication drawn by theorists such as Harold Innis, Eric Havelock, Marshall McLuhan, or Northrop Frye. The questions here have been focused on how to bring one together by means of the exercise of power attacking nature in an effort to overcome the vast stretches of emptiness. It is not surprising that this has portrayed itself in the guise of the technological imperative; the dynamo that can obliterate space at whatever cost under the imperative of the 'faster the better'.

This has simultaneously shifted the basis of revolutionary activity found in political economy with its concern with the property right. Here property disappears into endless stretches of rocks, trees, lakes, plains, and blackflies, creating the new forms of domination that hold sway under the control of those able to communicate. Capital shifts its locus to the iconic level where the grandest visions, usually spawned in the form of a colonial consciousness take their toll on the lives of men and women who had the worst luck to work on the railroads or the canals or, in a more contemporary context, today's CBC.

For those like Innis, the power that generated the empire of communications, produced in the end a sense of melancholy. The overcoming of space sent him back again in his "Plea for Time" for the values of the old world. And even for such a thinker as Marshall McLuhan, who turned the essence of the human inside out in the outering of consciousness in the technological warp, the drawing together was a means of conversion to the Catholic vision. Life in the fast lane, not only for Innis and McLuhan but also for a thinker like George Grant, ends in the quandary of trying to recapture some sense of the civilized moment that the conquering of the wilderness should have held out. It is a fact for these thinkers that the technological mastery had been swallowed by the American imperialism which has come to dominate, and has then led to the destruction of both the means and the content of communication itself.

The end-point of this vision has joined the discourse so common now in the post-structuralist world. The way power, through modern societies, has attacked and destroyed the older notions of representational knowledge, puts an end to our ability to affix identity in the state or in economic life. Even the text upon which these thinkers have written has itself begun to disintegrate. Pleas for time or space at best seem to generate a nostalgia for the fixed, yet dead, life of a past era. Having mapped the landscape in terms of the extension of power, that power has succeeded in destroying the past and, even more so, the sense of any meaning in such symbolic structures as the nation-state. Even the spectacles in our large cities, whether they be buildings, museums, governments, universities, or banks, while holding the individual in the grip of the relational power which these institutions embody, have a curious meaninglessness to them when confronted with the disintegration of any real reason for being here. Naturally, life goes on. There is a mixture of cynicism and innocence reflected in the desire of so many of the younger generation to enter the practice of law or commerce. One enters the nexus of the power structure, yet with the view that it hardly touches one at all.

Power is in many ways the starting-point of any study. One begins with the fact that our language is a power-system that no longer supports the ready identification of concepts with things, or of identities with 'paths of righteousness' as set out in any of our disciplines. The power of the various social codes that has invaded our texts has shown that the simple fictions of the author and the subject are no longer useful as starting-points, however much they may indeed

still capture the attempt to find within ourselves the identity, in a creative sense, of western individualism.

The question may be recast in terms of whether one can
understand the dynamics of a technological society as the
creation of a new series of visions while understanding that
the imagination itself has become an *imaginaire* or 'fantasy' in
its own right. The solace for many has been to turn towards
the world of the artists and to see in the exercise of the
artistic imagination the ability to shatter the monolithic grip
of power. In Marshall McLuhan, the role of the artist is
explicit and, indeed, finds support within a Canadian experience when one looks towards the poets and painters
who have depicted our reality. Even the Group of Seven,
with its borrowed techniques from the European past, has
managed, in the hands of an artist like Lauren Harris, to
evoke a sense of the relationship of the individual to the
wilderness that becomes a counter-foil to the wilderness of
our cities.

Here is the privileging of the imagination and of speech
in the attempt by the artist to reach through the technological veil to a form of meaning. In many instances, art can
appropriate the technology in ways in which the seeming
endless nihilism of technique can be turned inside out to
create the values to govern a new social existence. The artist
is then cast in the role of the law-breaker, the exposer, the
prophet, or revolutionary. The model has the enormous
appeal for its long lineage back in the western tradition to
Plato's fear of the artist. It also provides us with the theoretical underpinning to privilege the artist. Yet even such a
view itself is a remnant of the romantic rebellion so often
associated with the jettison of God as a creative principle. One
turns in the pages of a writer like Albert Camus to the history
of the artistic rebellion linked to the historical rebellions
that created the modern world after the French Revolution.

So back to the question of whether communication
should not be viewed as an aspect of the imaginative creation
of new symbols and structures, and, in particular, whether
behind the contemporary privileging of the artists, is not the

field of imagination itself ? And one perhaps might go further, asserting that the struggle within North American society, and in particular in the representatives of Canadian thought, is one between the domination of the individual by the technological materialism which has led to the conquering of space, and the attempt to order an inner space in the individual through the power of the imaginative vision. It is a contest as to whether the imagination itself can swallow the technological dynamo and survive to tell the tale. In order to do this, one must go back to the basis of what the imaginative experience is — to look behind the poet, the artist — to see the word or the symbol. This is the realm where Northrop Frye has been at work. And so the question of whether or not Northrop Frye can provide a vision of the New World.

Northrop Frye's recognition in the New World has come about through his role as literary critic. Frye's work in the 1950's assembled in the *Anatomy of Criticism* in 1957 established him as one of the foremost critics in the New American criticism. The work signaled the end in Frye's mind of the perspective of the literary critic as a parasitical appendage to the sleeve of the artistic geniuses whose work was being analyzed. In this sense, Frye was undoubtedly right, for the history of the last 30 years has seen the growing ascendency of literary theory as not only an independent discipline from literature, but also one of the foremost sites of philosophical investigation.

The literary critic is no longer solely occupied with the craft of analyzing the literary text. The writer has come front and centre in the debate about the meaning of language itself. One can easily go through the list of literary theorists, ranging from Roland Barthes, Jacques Derrida, Jeffrey Hartmann, Fredric Jameson, Harold Bloom, and, of course, Northrop Frye himself, to attest to the great power of the movement stemming from literary criticism.

There is, however, an irony: for the starting-point of *Anatomy of Criticism* was the attempt to establish the literary critic in a discipline separate not only from literature, but from other disciplines. In fact, in much of Frye's writing, there has been the constant refrain of not confusing literary criticism with psychology, political science, philosophy, or religion. Yet, the neat division of the disciplines and bounded fields is, as Michel Foucault demonstrated so persuasively, merely the rule of another law of power. Frye's attempt in the *Anatomy of Criticism* to separate social from literary theory is something that he has difficulty sustaining. The most pointed example of this can be found in Frye's *The Great Code,* the study of the Bible, which, as the title suggests, is not the Bible as literature but the Bible in relationship to literature; that is the Bible as a social and political document as much as a religious or literary document.

The use of words, in the corresponding imaginative structure that Frye paints, must extend beyond the field of literary criticism, as the history of literary criticism has shown. The perspective adopted in this study will be concerned with Frye as the mapper of a mythological universe that underlies the use of words in the western tradition.

Frye began each of his major studies of the poets or writers in the western tradition with the view that their works constituted an imaginative whole. This imaginative whole was structured by the previous works in the western tradition; thus the view throughout Frye's work is that each poet, each writer is recreating the same story which, in its essence, is the story set out in the Bible. I see no reason not to begin with Frye's model of how one should approach the works of a writer: that is to say, that the works of Northrop Frye must be taken as a whole in themselves. We begin with the assumption that they constitute an imaginative unity. This unity must be seen as following from Frye's attempt to recreate a basic mythological structure as he finds it in the western tradition, and to the extent that he believes his work goes beyond this, in the structure of human experience.

Frye's writings are prolific; some twenty or more books and numerous articles, an erudition that few in the twentieth century have been able to match. On one level, each work is merely an attempt to locate a poet or writer in the tradition of western literature. The author of these studies, Northrop Frye, completely disappears in letting the poet's images speak on behalf of the western tradition. Indeed going through the corpus of Frye's work, one might say, following many modern critics that there is no author called Northrop Frye. You cannot see him aside from the odd glimpse where he expresses an opinion outside of what he believes to be the canon of scientific judgments on the literary works. In this sense, Frye is a pre-eminently modern writer. He epitomizes the loss of the subject and the author of a text. Yet, it is also clear that, taken together, the texts themselves combine to form an extended commentary on the western imagination. It may be likened to a long play in which the actors, rather than fictional characters, are the literary figures. Presented before us, will be the likes of William Blake, John Milton, William Shakespeare, Edmund Spencer, Oswald Spengler, and a cast of hundreds of others. Frye is in each one of these individuals to such an extent that it is almost impossible in his work to separate the author who is being commented on from the writer of the text. Terry Eagleton in his commentary, *Literary Theory*, made the rather unusual remark that "Northrop Frye does exist."[2] This is profoundly mistaken: at the deepest level, Northrop Frye may be seen to be the mouthpiece through whom the tradition is articulating itself.

Frye's modernism is even more deeply rooted than his own disappearance from the text as an author. His conception of the western tradition as a mythological universe rests upon a view that life is an expression of energy that takes on the forms of literary and political creations. At the base of Frye's writing is a conception of bio-power which extends in a vast field throughout history. Power is depicted as energy which creates the forms of literary work that appear through the pens of the artists and poets. This represents Frye's attempt to get beyond the categories of time and space, good and evil, or any of the categories of law that constitute the power structure of the western mind. It is a profoundly idealistic conception and undoubtedly reflects Frye's religious belief. Yet, outside of this personal assumption, there is also a very strong link to the conception of the word being the locus of power common to the conception of the individual as a communicative being. The tracing of this energy gives rise to the structural studies which led to Frye's identification with structuralism. On the other hand, Frye through the very nature of his enterprise deconstructs the structures from one artist to the next showing the many codes that emanate from the experience of life as they are handed down in the various great works of art. The content of the works of art are yet other forms of the energy of the creative principle at the base of his system.

When one considers Frye's work in the social realm, it must be matched by the other great principle that he identifies in the structure of the western tradition and more particularly with the study of the Bible. To the extent that Frye retains Christian imagery, the creative energy becomes analogous to the conception of freedom implicit in the choice, made symbolically in the Garden of Eden, resulting in humanity's fall. It is this fall, which is generated as a result of the exercise of freedom, that creates the great paradigm of law. This leads to the consequent judgment of humanity ultimately outside of time and space. Law then becomes the governing metaphor in Frye's world for human society, and, in particular, sets out the tension between freedom and justice. Much of Frye's social vision is tied up with the conception of the social contract as an emanation from the fundamental need in a society to bring judgment to bear on freedom's actions.

Frye, then, may be seen as one of the great defenders of liberalism in the modern world. It is a defense rooted not only in the conception of the Bible that Frye holds, but in the affinity of much of his thought for the political and social vision of a writer like John Milton. Frye will be identified more particularly with the social and political philosophy underlying. Thomas Hobbes' conception of man as a power seeker. It is quite true that Frye has little time for the royalist metaphor, but behind Hobbes' authoritarianism lie the roots of the identification made by liberalism between the individual and the class-structure developed upon the individual's exercise of power. For Hobbes, as much as for Frye, judgments in their final sense are human creations, and relate to the world of enforcement symbolized by law where the desires are channelled by what Frye will call later the "emergency authority of society" against the freedom of the individual.

Frye's defense of liberalism retains, however, the element that society must have a concern for culture in a fashion that informs it of the uses it should be making of freedom. This establishes the ambiguity, in Frye's work in the political realm between Frye the revolutionary, who sides with the visions of Milton and Blake against the *status quo,* and, on the other hand, Frye's allegiance to the social contract theories of John Locke. Frye sides with Locke's view that the world of sensual expression epitomized by Locke's philosophy must be honoured in a social system that is to avoid the problems of anarchy and violence. Frye's attempt at a social vision establishes his case as much against Blake as for Locke in the overall synthesis that he is attempting to make of the various positions in the western tradition. One must bear this in mind when reading Frye's work on a poet and critic like T.S. Eliot whose thumbnail sketch as a royalist, conservative and Catholic stands antithetical to the thumbnail sketch of Frye as a republican, liberal and Protestant.

A similar relationship can be drawn to the works of Marshall McLuhan. McLuhan taught at St. Michael's College, only a short distance from where Frye taught at Victoria College. Here was another version of what might be called the two solitudes or, as George Woodcock calls Frye and McLuhan, the 'two ornaments' of the University of Toronto. McLuhan's concern for the outering of the sensory network seems to be in marked contrast to Frye's concern with the inner freedom of the individual's existence outside the dimensions of time and space. Yet, even here, Frye's ability to absorb an antithetical position within his larger scheme is attempted. McLuhan's concern for the writings of James Joyce and the poetry of T.S. Eliot and Ezra Pound, along with Frye's preference for a Milton or a Blake, are both swallowed in his conception of man as a maker of forms. Whether these forms lean towards the conservative, the radical or the liberal are less important messages for Frye than the fact that they are energy and motion, which will map itself over time and space in any number of combinations. All of these in Frye's vocabulary are recreations of the original charge to individuals as speaking beings.

In many ways, Frye's work relates back to the epistemological framework of Immanuel Kant where the imaggination creates the categories through which we understand the world. Frye, no less than Kant, sees time and space as constructions of the mind, and these constructions are likened to the forms through which individuals then live their existence. Frye, writing in the modern period, does not make these identifications with the Newtonian absolutes of time and space in the fashion Kant did. Frye rather is closer to the conception of field theory that characterizes more modern descriptions of physics. In a lecture given in 1983, Frye chose as his title "Literature as the Critique of Pure Reason" playing on the word critique used in its sense as the basis of 'pure reason' and also in a sense of being critical of the western tradition's use of reason as it emanates from the enlightenment. At the core of reason for Frye is unreason, the unreason of the individual who participates in the recreation of the mythological universes that have been common to human existence wherever it is found. Hence liberalism with its rule of law rests in Frye's view not upon a foundation of a reasonable vision of the individual entering the social contract, but rather a contract that for Frye can, under the aegis of freedom, be redrawn in many ways by the recreative imagination.

The redrawing of the social contract by the creative imagination holds within it the tension between the claims to reason and unreason that leads men in Frye's world constantly to the propagations of mythologies. Frye's work joins that of a former colleague from Victoria College, Eric Havelock, who began his studies by looking at the progress of science from the pre-Socratics as a counter-tradition to that of the theories of Plato and Aristotle. For Frye and Havelock, the early development of the western tradition hinges very fundamentally on the identification of technology and reason in the scientific enterprise that orders the energy emanating from the creative individual. For Havelock, this energy is characterized by technology itself and is seen by him as a uniformly good counter-current to the philosophical destruction wrought in the western tradition by Hegelian philosophies. Frye, while sharing much of Havelock's cold-war mentality, nevertheless, sees the technological imperative to be at odds with the creative imagination.

It is the growing split between progress as the unveiling of identity, and progress as the destruction of that identity that brings Frye's thought to a place where technological visions are nightmarish spectres of a society out of control. In *The Educated Imagination*, Frye's series of talks for the CBC Radio, he draws as his conclusion the vision of contemporary cities as technological skyscrapers poised in a fashion similar to that of Babel to destroy any semblance of communication among human beings. The task as set out in this radio broadcast is one of reeducating society to what, in Frye's opinion, it already knows from its mythological heritage. This fashions the view that runs throughout so much of Frye's work that education and culture must attempt to find the depowered site where the 'poets can be heard.'

Frye's perspective on the modern world will be to overcome what he perceives to be the fallen nature of the social realm as it has been given to us. The New World is symbolically the bush garden for Frye, or to use one of his frequent translations, a reenacted form of paradise where one can replay the human drama that has been set out for Europe in Milton's *Paradise Lost* or in Blake's *Four Zoas*. In Frye's terminology, we live in an era predominantly described by the myth of decline which, of course, emanates from the very structure of myths such as the Garden of Eden. This positions us at a point in our history where we can again engage in a secular rise associated with the birth of a new world.

Frye's treatment of nature becomes central to the basis of his vision. It also brings one back to the core of Frye's liberalism and the compromise in his thought. Frye's thought oscillates between two conceptions of nature, one as the state of peace, the other, the state of war. This contradiction is part of the liberal tradition found at its origins in, for example, John Locke's *Two Treatises of Government.* It characterizes the incorporation of the contradictory aspects of the social into the concept of nature.[3] With Frye, there is a tension in his ontology between energy as the technological will and energy as the will to the peaceable kingdom. This tension gives rise to the compromise underlying Frye's case for a technological humanism, or, as I have called it, 'improved binoculars.' This produces the flawed vision of the liberal imagination.

The starting-point for developing Frye's vision is its end in the theories that he sketches in the study of the Bible. The various symbols, myths, and archetypes that Frye analyzes in his last work bear a striking similarity to the themes and interpretive keys that he uses in his early study of William Blake. Thus, I turn to *The Great Code* in the next chapter to set out the theoretical principles upon which Frye's system of thought rests. For, once having understood the basis of the sensual and experiential life as it is portrayed in the various falls that Frye believes underlies our current situation, we will be able to see the New World vision that Frye wishes us to have at the end of his work.

2

Energy Without Alienation

But what the Bible gives us is not so much a cosmology as a vision of upward metamorphosis, of the alienated relation of man to nature transformed into a spontaneous and effortless life — not effortless in the sense of being lazy or passive, but in the sense of being energy without alienation.

The Great Code[1]

America: A Prophecy

It is clear that the great good book is in trouble. The most fundamental work of our culture is no longer read, thought about, or remotely considered by the majority of individuals. While it is true that one still occasionally finds copies of the Bible in hotel rooms in the western hemisphere, it becomes increasingly more difficult to believe that this is part of a great conspiracy, or, if you prefer, an awakening of the population to the Bible and its message. We are in a realm now of the truly dead sea scrolls.

To a writer like Northrop Frye, this is the single most important fact of cultural life in the modern age. It is the break with the past that destroys our ability to read and ultimately our ability to express ourselves. It is the basis of the human identity crisis. A resurrection is called for, yet one must contend with the fact that society finds increasingly more relevance in rock videos than in church appearances. This leaves only one way out. These videos with their concern for forms of bondage, violence, transformations or transmigration must be seen to be part of the same concerns as that of the Bible. The Bible must be stripped of its religious kernel, and broken of its political power, not just turned into a movie. Then we will experience its ubiquity: or so the story goes.

Recognizing that Frye, if he watches rock videos does not speak of them, must rest his case upon the assertion that the mythological structure of the western tradition, at its most profound level, is the Bible. The Bible inevitably will reappear in cultural forms whether they be high or low, to use vocabulary that Frye is not comfortable with. Frye, in his own way, is out to save the Bible.

We are thus presented with a paradox that will recur constantly in Frye's work. The paradox stems from the fact that the most important elements of our tradition, the Bible, Shakespeare, Blake, Milton or any other artists you care to name, are virtually the most unknown aspects of contemporary society. Society has for Frye come to the point of being beyond forgetting, of not even knowing any longer of the existence of the works that inform the vocabulary used by modern society. The twentieth century has an odd affinity to John Locke's view expressed in *The Essay on Human Understanding* that the human mind is a *tabula rasa*. We are blank sheets of paper increasingly ignorant of the origins of our own thoughts. To express this in a different form, the individual is alienated from the basic life source: an alienation that is a part of the biblical myth as identified with the fall. Modern individualism begins with the fall into a state of ignorance and anxiety.

In European cities, the evidence of the alienation of human energy is everywhere in the buildings and museums that form a constant reminder of the interweaving of time in space that underlies the culture itself. Gone is the urgency felt by a writer like John Milton who believed that the recreation underway in the English revolution might lead England to the New Albion. This moment has passed for England. Similarly, on the European continent, the long series of revolutions beginning with the French revolution signals the failure of that culture to create a new society. The serpent of the Garden of Eden becomes most appropriately the symbol of Europe that has lost its vitality — Europe whose knowledge of good and evil has ended in the nihilism of the post-Nietzschean world. At once, the most "cultured" part of the modern world, Europe in the twentieth century is no longer capable of the prophetic vision. Europe is caught in a "nihilistic psychosis", as Frye suggests in a retrospective comment in 1969, that engulfs both the "reactionary and radical"[2] forces alike. It can no longer be the ground from which such visions will emanate. In the end, thinkers as diverse as Blake and Hegel must look to the Americas for the prophecy to come. And, indeed, so does Frye.

The loss of energy of the Old World is precisely the reason why Frye must turn to the New World for his understanding of the continuing relevance of the biblical tradition. The knights sent out to the New World, even at the time of Blake's writing of *America* in the 1790's, had fallen off their horses in the old country. It was left to others involved with the technology of canoes and trains to give rise to new and different social orders. For it is in the New World that we are not encumbered by the spectres of the past. In other words, the serpent-dragon of Europe must be slain in the renewal of the Americas.

> The dragon-killing is thus a drama both of the reviving powers of nature and of a freedom from some kind of social oppression. Putting the two things together, we get the principle that such a revolution as is occurring in America is a natural renewal of life in society, and that it therefore does not happen irrationally, but at a definite time, like the dawn and the spring.[3]

When one looks, as Frye does, upon the vast expanse of space in the New World, one can only be struck by the similarity of the physical reality to the basic metaphor of the biblical condition in the garden. To Frye, the Bible con-

stantly speaks to the "younger" generation; that is, to those
with the energy to seek a new world. Thus, the Bible is pre-
eminently a modern work in its concern for the relation of
the individual to nature. Read symbolically, it is a guide to
achieve a better society.

The image I have of Frye's Bible is perhaps comparable
to the types of gardening volumes prominent in the cata-
logues of book-of-the-month. It offers the ways and means
to turn one's rather out of control backyard into a flowering
paradise: a vision depicted later in this study by the Canadian
artist Marion Wagschal in her scathing criticism of the
modern world. The Bible, for Frye, is the "wilderness hand
book", a type of companion piece to the record of our early
experience living in the New World found in the diaries of a
Suzanna Moodie or in the writings of a Catherine Parr Traill.
The North American experience starts as the experience of
innocence associated with those who are faced with the
founding of a new social order; a social order that begins
with the fall of Adam. The Bush Garden is what has become
of the Garden of Eden. It is a garden that no longer exists in
Europe.

As such, Frye represents in a more fundamental fashion
than contemporary theorists in Europe, the inheritance of
the western tradition. For it is precisely because the tradition could no longer live in the European context that it
was forced to move to the New World and find there its
articulation. Frye stands almost uniquely positioned to
argue for the continuance of the tradition precisely because
the circumstances surrounding the development of the New
World are so much akin to the basic struggle epitomized by
the biblical concern.

Much of European thought claims that the tradition has
ended. This is the case, whether it be from the conservative
position of a Martin Heidegger who posits the end of
metaphysics, or Jacques Derrida who counsels the abandonment of the logocentric world, or Roland Barthes' nostalgia
for the loss of the tradition in *Camera Lucida* where he tries to
see in the faded pictures of the past what is left of his own
civilization. All are, in many ways, foreign to the project that

Frye holds. There is no "nostalgia for the absolute", to use George Steiner's phrase, precisely because the past is continually being recreated in the New World in the tension between the alienation of the creative energies in technology and their materialization in the life of activity envisaged by Frye's Bible.

In following these paths, I am led in two directions, which are complementary in Frye's ultimate project to reconstitute the understanding of ourselves. The first, which will be dealt with below, is to see Frye's Bible in terms of his claim that it forms a universal structure of the human mind as found in western civilization. This is Frye as the inheritor of the western tradition. The second route is to follow Frye down the path set out in the Canadian poet E.J. Pratt's *Toward the Last Spike*. Here we will see how the mythological universe unveils itself in the North American experience as it works its way through the technological empire of the railroad in the attempt to recreate the garden, or as Pratt expresses it, the same world "except for little differences of speed"[4].

Behold Now Behemoth

What precedes Frye's *The Great Code* is the William Blake print entitled "Behold now Behemoth which I made with thee." The print depicts God in place in the heavens pointing towards the natural world where two creatures are shown. The one is a partially humanized creature ressembling an elephant, the behemoth, standing above the seas. The second represents a serpent that is coiled in the sea but with the head looking upwards to the elephant-man. This central image of the naturalized world in which humanity is half beast and half human is one that recurs throughout Frye's work and, in particular, influences his interpretation of the Bible as humanity striving towards the higher form of life epitomized by God in the heavens. This basic image captures the movement of consciousness inside humanity from the vegetative state upwards to the fully human, and then finally to the divine apocalypse represented by the heavens beyond space and time. If the Bible contributes anything to Frye, it

William Blake, *Behemoth and Leviathan*

is this image of humanity moving from the fallen state towards a higher level which may be called civilization.

Thus, the enormous importance of the Bible is that it provides us with the account of origins and ends, and a dynamic of existence between the two. We, of course, have never been at the beginning. Frye is at pains to say the Bible is a symbolic and analogical rendering of existence which in itself is not susceptible to rational explanation. Nor for that matter would we expect to find God up in the heavens; a fact, of course, that no one needed the space program to demonstrate. As obvious as these "facts" are, they are, nevertheless, central to the understanding of Frye's position. We come from 'nowhere', and we are going 'nowhere', from 'energy to energy' one might say rather than from 'dust to dust.' We are engaged in a pursuit ultimately of things outside of time and space of which the only access is through the imagination. The Bible, then, becomes the book of our imaginative universe.

The imagination is a well-known aspect of Frye's work which appears as a main theme in his talks and his writings.

The focus on the imagination is a central category underlying existence on earth. Descriptions of Frye have focussed on the role of the imagination in depicting the apocalyptic vision. This will be commented on later. Yet, of equal force is the fact that in Frye's cosmology, humanity is still rooted on earth. We remain for our existence and time here within that globe depicted by the serpent and the elephant. The world that we must encounter is that ruled by the Behemoth or the Great Leviathan. What separates Frye from traditional religion is precisely the point expressed so cogently by Samuel Beckett in his play, *The End Game*, where he says, "you're on earth, there's no cure for that!"[5] In reading Frye, one must never lose sight of the irony which he detects in the writings of the modern age, and from which he is scarcely free.

The Blake etching also enables us to understand that Frye's analysis of Blake's work in *Fearful Symmetry,* at the beginning of his career, encounters his later concerns with the Bible proper in *The Great Code*. As I will show later, this is a tension between Blake and Frye. Frye plays the role of the latter-day Blake by attempting to "swallow" Blake in the same fashion that Blake attempted to "swallow" Milton. Or to express it in a different fashion, Frye attempts to recreate the poem *America.*

Therefore, the Bible will be taken pre-eminently as commentary on the human condition given by Frye outside of a traditional religious context. It is a commentary that will provide the basic images of the individual, society and of nature in the tension between the claim of the individual to live an unalienated existence or 'energy without alienation', and the fact that one must live in an alienated world. The Bible depicts humanity's struggle for freedom which begets the domination of a society created out of the fall; a society that I have linked in this study with the technological world. This struggle provides Frye not only with a sense of the essence of humanity, but also with a methodology that allows him to interpret how men and women transform the human condition into one of true community. This leads to a discussion of what humanity is by nature as revealed to us in the Bible and how this basic nature provides the hermeneutical key to the understanding of the "words" of men and women that follow.

These words are inextricably bound to the two great images in the Bible; that of the law and that of the subsequent judgment against those who have exercised their inner freedom. Thus the Bible must be read from the perspective of the Behemoth. The Bible, for Frye, is precisely the account of the judgment against humanity and how this judgment has structured social existence. The Bible is the original social contract that has been breached. This breach constitutes the original loss of freedom.

This will bring us to the core of Frye's liberalism: his distrust of the law and judgment, and his defense of the individual against the great codes of society and of the imaginative world. The role of judgment extends not only to the disciplining of the thief who stole the fire of the gods and turned it into the technological imperative. It also extends into the realm of the artist where aesthetic judgments suffice to exile the artist as mad or threaten to throw the social order into the anarchy of the primordial state of nature.

Frye's great alter ego in this struggle is Aristotle. Frye has his roots in the Aristotelian tradition where the basic conception of the individual as a physical being, as a being infused with energy, meets head on the discipline of politics as the rule of law. This signals Frye's own ambiguity when faced with the creative artist as the law-breaker. It creates in Frye a deep sense that liberal society in the end must reflect the pluralism which denies to any one vision the social power to bring about the new. It is, in the end, Aristotle's rule of law, an acceptance of the Behemoth.

The Great Code of Art

Frye tells us at the beginning of his study of the Bible that the title, *The Great Code,* was taken from William Blake's reference to the Bible as "The Great Code of Art." In the universe of William Blake art is an expression used to describe the fundamental experience of humanity. For

Blake, this fundamental experience can be identified with the creative imagination. This sets Blake's animus against the epistemological theories of John Locke which stressed the individual's role as a receiver of sense impressions in the material world rather than as a creator. For Blake, the reflective theory of consciousness stood at the opposite pole of the creative imagination.

When Frye picks up Blake's phrase, he interestingly enough leaves out the reference to art and reformulates Blake's thoughts in terms of the Bible as a "great code." To see the Bible as a code of art would be to place the Bible within the confines of literature. This, as we can see from Frye's title, he is reluctant to do. The study is the Bible and literature but, more fundamentally, it is the study of the preconditions that underlie the creative imagination of Blake and the reflective consciousness of Locke. Behind both stands, for Frye, energy itself. Energy stands for what is, as much as for what ought to be. We can see that theoretically Frye attempts to straddle both science and art, resting upon the factual realm of Locke and Newton as much as the creative realm of Blake and Milton as a way of reflecting the true nature of the existence of humanity.

Frye's view of energy may, as a consequence, be likened to that of an onion. One peels off the outer skins of science, technology, and culture to find the theoretical justifications that emanate from each of the major thinkers in the western tradition. And behind that, yet again, one expects for Frye to find the core as the vision of the Bible. In terms of the development of Frye's position, the rings surrounding the core are always those of Blake followed by Milton. The core is always the pure potentiality of the unrealized energy of creation. This is Frye's ontological assumption.

This may be illustrated by a return to *Fearful Symmetry* to the initial starting-point of Blake's conception, as Frye quotes him from the *Marriage of Heaven and Hell:* "Energy is the only life, and is from the Body; and Reason is the bound or outward circumference of Energy."[6] Life on earth, under the Great Leviathan, is first and foremost energy which is only bounded when imagination as energy is incorporated in form. This conception of active energy accounts for the highest levels of artistic creation and of love and wonderment in Blake's system. Again, quoting from *Fearful Symmetry:*

> Ultimately, our attitude to what we see is one of mental conquest springing from active energy . . . The highest possible state, therefore, is not the union of lover and beloved, but of creator and creature, of energy and form.[7]

The translation of energy into form becomes the principal activity of civilization in its attempt to turn the state of nature or the primordial state into that of a cultivated, civilized society. It is this activity which establishes in Frye's world the linkage between nature as energy or "physis", and society or civilization. One flows from the other through the application of form to the basic life force of humanity. We can also see from the period when Frye was writing *Fearful Symmetry* that he had in his mind the strong linkage between Milton's work and Blake's.

> Milton's "liberty" is practically the same thing as Blake's imagination, and whenever Milton talks about reason he means it in the sense of the "bound or outward circumference of Energy" which liberty supplies. Liberty for Milton is the total release of the whole man, and his main effort in defining it is to break down the partitions in which the timid and cautious attempt to keep its various aspects separate. That is, the "Christian liberty" of the theologians is not a different thing from political liberty; and the "liberty to know and utter" inevitably expands into the liberty to love.[8]

The similarity in starting-point between Frye's Blake and Frye's Milton was reiterated again by Frye in a later set of essays which he wrote in 1963 and titled *The Return of Eden.* If anything in this work, Frye is more deliberate in his association of energy with the basis of freedom in Milton's work. In reference to Milton's *The Christian Doctrine,* Frye defines an action as "the expression of the energy of a free and conscious being."[9] From this follows, as I shall show later, the conception of the fall as the surrendering of the power to act where humanity no longer has the energy given to it by God. We also see in Frye's description of Milton the repetition of the very important identification of energy with form. To quote again *The Return of Eden:*

> After the fall, the hierarchy implanted by God in the human soul is not merely upset, but reversed. Appetite now moves into the top place in the human soul, and by doing so it ceases to be appetite and is transformed into passion, the drive toward death. The appetites are a part of the creation, and like every other part of the creation they are an energy which seeks its fulfillment in form.[10]

Frye's reading of the tradition then extends the view that humanity is basically energy to the view that humanity is energy seeking form. From Blake, we know that this at once gives the role of the creative artist. From Locke, we will be able to see that humanity is also given the role of the scientific form-maker. And finally from Milton, we see that these forms are inherently political in nature given the exercise of freedom.

In a religious sense, this defines the relationship of humanity to God. Frye again, commenting on Milton's works, believes that Milton paints the picture of the creator who moves downwards towards humanity releasing the energy of music and poetry to create the form most powerfully symbolized by the Word. Humanity, on the other hand, is required to move upwards towards God "by obeying the inner law of its own being, its *telos* or chief end, which is always and at all levels the glorifying of God."[11]

This is a particularly fertile passage for it provides us with the basis of a number of concepts that we will meet later in Frye's work. First, the role of the literary critic has just

received divine sanction as the observer and cataloguer of
the various forms created in the interaction between God
and humanity. The political dimension of this role will be
described later. Second, in this scheme of things, there is no
direct challenge of God by the creating of artistic works for
all things, all forms, are already known to God in the beginning. This will signal the movement in Frye's work away
from creation to recreation as the primary activity of energy.
It is also sufficient enough to turn Frye from romantic
rebellion which he considers to be at the base of the Marxian
revolutionary model. Third, we can see how very much the
struggle in this traditional sense is an inner struggle which
will be worked out in the outer world, but whose final
resolution is one of inner spirit.

Finally, the forms that energy take capture the essence of
humanity's spiritual dimension. First and foremost, this is
symbolized by the Word. Taken in a religious sense this is, of
course, the Word of God. The intellectual forms may also be
seen to be the primary concepts which humanity creates in
its understanding of the world. In particular, it is important
to see that Frye appropriates Milton's sense that the energy
of God takes on the form on earth of the categories of time
and space. To refer again to *The Return of Eden* Frye comments on the abstractions in *Paradise Lost* in the following
manner:

> Third, and most important, they abstract the two
> aspects of God's creative power, energy and form,
> into the categories which we know as time and
> space. Thus in the later demonic theology, time
> and space are the official creative forces of the
> world. [12]

Frye's Bible becomes the form which God's energy, through
recreation, takes in the world. The forms of time and space
signify the mortality of man and woman brought about by
the fall, seen as the lapse of energy into the passivity of the
inertial state. This also provides an agenda for Frye in
looking at the way in which the Word spreads out through

our history as philosophy, literature, art and politics. This also provides a plan for looking at how the Word structures a relationship to God. From the Word, we then go to the sentence, or in a rather expanded sense, to literature itself, as a way of understanding the order of Words and hence the order of our thinking in the western tradition. Then, finally, we will pass into the state of the fall captured culturally for us in Spengler's *The Decline of the West,* as I will discuss later. I turn now to Frye's understanding of God as the Word.

The Dead See

At the beginning of *The Great Code,* Frye gives us his key to understanding God's disappearance from the modern world. God has ended; buried in a form of language and thought that has now become quite dead. This language is the language of modern society. Frye sees this language giving rise to the traditional view of God in terms of an object or a thing represented, most often in terms of the father figure. This tradition of representing is at an end. It ends in the rubble surrounding the demolished houses of God. Thinking must go elsewhere.

Frye, from the perspective of the grammarian, recreates his conception of God as a verb rather than a noun. Behold the resurrection! Here is how he expresses it:

> That is, we might come closer to what is meant in the Bible by the word "God" if we understood it as a verb, and not a verb of simple asserted existence but a verb implying a process accomplishing itself. This would involve trying to think our way back to a conception of language in which words were words of power, conveying primarily the sense of forces and energies rather than analogues of physical bodies.[13]

Frye, in rejecting representational epistemologies, establishes a relational conception of being predicated, as I have shown, on the view of the human as energy. In *The Great Code,* he moves further than in his studies of Milton and Blake by establishing God on the ground of energy. This energy, joining the view expressed earlier, is a relational power carried by language. Discourse becomes the site of power.

Frye, in using this definition, also turns back towards the conception of the verb "to be" as presencing as it existed in the tradition prior to the development of the Platonic forms. In this sense, to be is to be present to something. In that presencing, one establishes a relationship between individuals. That is, there is at once an assertion of being, but an assertion of being reflecting power or "life force." This line of argument will draw Frye closer to Martin Heidegger, creating what in the Canadian discourse may be a new oddity of the "tory touch in liberalism."

Despite all of this, the current discourse about God and power remains locked into the representational forms. Frye goes on to say, in the same quotation:

> But it would also be oddly contemporary with post-Einsteinian physics, where atoms and electrons are no longer thought of as things but rather as traces of processes. God may have lost his function as the subject or object of a predicate, but may not be so much dead as entombed in a dead language.[14]

The release of God then implies a release from the "dead language" which in turn releases human energy. Frye restores a conception of *logos* as a creative act that both posits the new and honours the old. Human activity then becomes identified not with a preset form or ideological conception of what God or truth or science or art may have it, but rather the very process of shaping energy into a manifold number of forms or concepts. This leads us to the dynamic of human activity for Frye in the creation by energy of new languages or new forms which are forever then becoming objectified and set against the individual as objects. This gives rise, as I will show in the next section, to Frye's history of language and his attempt to free language from the entombing characteristics that have become associated with the conception of God.

Escape from the Prison-House of Language

The Bible provided the imaginative codes or forms which shaped human energy into the works of art, culture and technology and which finally shaped God. This is fundamental to Frye's study of the Bible, which is not, I repeat, the study of the religious significance of the Bible. We have lost that. The Bible no longer speaks to us because we no longer understand the language. Thus Frye proceeds to sweep the sands from the tomb. His approach to the Bible is partly that of the literary critic, but only part. The role of the literary critic is a mask that Frye puts on while he is really engaged in the more fundamental question of how one understands the experiences one has of the world. Frye's own title, *The Bible and Literature*, is misleading: there are no separate universes. For the Bible is the order of words that provides the keys and the codes to understanding, whether from a religious or literary view.

From this vantage point, it is not surprising to see that Frye's approach to the Bible is really a description of the way in which words have been used throughout the western tradition. One will find many examples in the corpus of Frye's work of his attempting to put an epistemological structure on the way in which we use language. In Robert Denham's *Northrop Frye's Critical Method,*[15] we see these different categories painstakingly and methodically established. But this is really the labour of Sisyphus. One is reminded of the types of categories developed by Kant in his philosophical system, where he attempted in his tables to provide an exhaustive set of concepts for the foundation of knowledge. We know, in retrospect, that Kant's list was no more complete than perhaps any other list of such categories would be. This is certainly also true with Frye. His inventiveness for making new terms or borrowing other people's terms with new definitions is legendary. Take, for example, his view of myth which is given at least a half dozen definitions depending on the context of Frye's writing. One can conclude from this that the interpreter's art has a conventionality about it, although, as Frye would hasten to point out, it should not be confused with an arbitrary ordering of this subject-matter.

However, it would hardly advance us very far to see that Frye is inconsistent or, even for that matter, contradictory in the use of various systems unless, indeed, we share the premise that there exists an absolute set of logical categories. It would be more profitable to see that Frye really is deconstructing the codes behind various works, and has recognized the multiplicity of structures that can be overlaid on experience. The limitations of Frye's approach will become apparent later, having to do with his selection of the code of a scientific critic. But even here, I shall show that Frye's work tries to escape from this prison house through the recognition that in categorizing the order of words, he must move beyond the compliance of his scientism as it is reflected in literary criticism.

While the influences on Frye's methodology are spread out throughout the various authors that he has treated in the western tradition, the history of language is pre-eminently indebted to Vico. Frye's Vico makes his appearance many times in his works, but nowhere more importantly than in the first part of *The Great Code.* I turn now to Vico's zoology.

Vico's Giants

Frye, in light of the Scienza Nova, *recovers through Blake that naturally poetic language of the giants, and formulates it as a universal poetic, a grammar of archetypes . . .*

Criticism in the Wilderness[16]

Vico's "new science" depended upon the recognition of the various cycles or stages in history identified by Vico with the development of poetic imagination. Frye, following Vico, identifies the three cycles as follows:

> a mythical age, or age of gods; a heroic age, or age of an aristocracy; and an age of the people, after which there comes a *ricorso* or return that starts the whole process over again.[17]

Frye then goes on to state that each of these ages produces a special kind of language which he calls the hieroglyphic, the hieratic, and the demotic. Frye's attraction to Vico's scheme is two-fold. The first is that Vico's new science is premised upon what, for Frye, is the fact of the mythological universe. As he states in the introduction to *The Great Code:*

> Man lives, not directly or nakedly in nature like the animals, but within a mythological universe, a body of assumptions and beliefs developed from his existential concerns.[18]

Humanity's initial response to the natural world and to life itself is to understand it in terms of a mythology as opposed to a rationality.

Perhaps greater significance lies in the second point that he draws from Vico, that the whole cycle is not a linear progression, but rather is a *ricorso*, a return again at the end to the type of mythological structures that formed the beginning. We can see here, as elsewhere, the origins of Frye's own tension between the myth of progress as one form of the mythological universe that has been appropriated by the development of technology, and the basic structure of mythology which for Frye is always circular.

Frye will not go as far as a critic such as John O'Neill in using Vico as a way of resurrecting the body after the attack on it of the scientific rationality of the twentieth– and nineteeth centuries. Yet Vico's notion of the *gentes* or nation reappears under Frye's internationalism. He shares with Vico the sense that the order of language determines our relationships at the level of political power, and hence that the history of language cannot be separated from the history of the political as it outlines itself primarily through the history of war. In Frye's vision, Vico's giants have large heads, and rather wizened bodies: a near inverse of the old dinosaur.

While Frye sees a similarity between the categories that he develops from Vico and the basic categories he used in the *Anatomy of Criticism,* I have chosen the former set, for they extend beyond the discipline of literary theory. As Frye points out, the various categories are all linked by a common power or energy which then leads to his concept of subject and object. The key to Frye's development of the categories lies with his sense that "only metaphor can express in language the sense of an energy common to subject and object."[19] It is the various forms of this energy that would provide us with the development of the western tradition.

Frye identifies the first phase of language, the poetic or hieroglyphic phase, predominantly with Greek literature before Plato and the pre-book cultures of the Near East. At the base of the use of words in this early phase is the attempt to have some power over the dynamic forces that make up the natural environment. These cultures chiefly identify various aspects of nature with the form of personality which, as we know, is translated into the various forms of "gods." Frye appears very close in his use of the poetic to that found in Horkheimer's and Adorno's study in the *Dialectic of Enlightenment.* Premised here is a fundamental unity of humanity with nature, hence the desire to personify the natural world. Thus, Frye shares the view that ultimately humanity must come to some reuniting with nature which has fundamentally been alienated through the rapacious development of technological energies.

This stands in marked contrast to Eric Havelock's discussion in *The Liberal Temper of Greek Politics*[20] where nature's energy is considered as technology. In the pre-Socratic world, technology has a human face. The return, however, to this stage of the state of nature is only contemplated by Frye in an anagogic vision unlike Havelock's view that technology is always humanizing. Yet as an ideal type for

Frye, a humanized technology will reappear throughout the images that Frye creates and which are referred to as 'improved binoculars' later in this study.

Frye's identification of the second form of language, the hieratic, is made with the Platonic tradition. Again, this accords with many commentators who see the development of written culture's ascendancy over the oral with Plato and the tradition that follows. In common with others, this is marked by the ascendancy of the conceptual or the idea as separated from the realm of sensual experience. In an epistemological sense, the subjects and the objects are now becoming separated, although the separation is often conceptualized in the form of a mirror or reflection. Here is how Frye expresses in *The Great Code:*

> The basis of expression here is moving from the metaphorical, with its sense of identity of life or power or energy between man and nature ("this is that"), to a relationship that is rather metonymic ("this is put for that"). Specifically, words are "put for" thoughts, and are the outward expressions of an inner reality. But this reality is not merely "inside". Thoughts indicate the existence of a transcendent order "above", which only thinking can communicate with and which only words can express. The metonymic language is, or tends to become, analogical language, a verbal imitation of a reality beyond itself that can be conveyed most directly by words.[21]

Frye characterizes this period in three ways. First, it is the beginning of continuous prose as opposed to the discontinuous aphorisms that characterize the pre-Socratics. Secondly, this prose can be conceived of on a dialectical basis in its attempt to form a transcendent world as opposed to sensual world that predominates in metaphorical language. And thirdly, the development of hieratic continuous prose allows for the development of monotheism in the place of the polytheistic world of nature. God comes into existence as the power which will be the means of controlling human society in its spiritual and temporal aspects.

It is tempting to follow Robert Denham in identifying Frye's position with the Platonic forms. There is, of course, some similarity to Frye's desire to see reality in terms of forms. And indeed to the extent that he shares an idealistic perspective, one must give some credence to this view. There is, however, a counterside to the Platonic elements in Frye which leads one to upset this identification. For Frye's political thought has been influenced by Karl Popper's analysis of Plato in *The Open Society and Its Enemies.* The Platonic regime is fundamentally antithetical to the liberal imagination, and this antipathy is centred upon the closure that the absolute forms have to thought and thinking. Frye agrees with Popper in seeing the dangers of the closure of the myths of the gods into the totalizing vision of one God. One can find throughout Frye's studies an unease with the total vision presented both philosophically or artistically. If there are forms in heaven, for Frye, they are more like clouds that take on various shapes depending on the winds.

Frye's concern with Plato is manifested in a number of other areas as well. He is acutely aware of the tension in the Platonic works between the role of the philosopher and that of the poet, and there certainly are times in which Frye believes that Plato becomes more the artist than the philosopher in the designs of the *Republic.* We will meet this tension later in the way in which Frye attempts to resolve the role of the philosopher in politics by having the literary critic displace the philosopher as the counsellor of the past and the prophet of the future. Frye's rejection of the philosopher-king and his later rejection of the Machiavellian counsellor brings his political position far closer to that of Martin Heidegger's fundamental view that being is articulated in language, but the arbiter of language is, for Frye, the literary critic.

The third phase of language, following Vico, is the demotic which Frye identifies with the language that holds sway in our current time. This form of language is antithetical to the first two in its rejection of allegorical or meta-

phorical elements. Frye also sees this language as antithetical to the very conception of the individual. This is the
language of the Great Leviathan, used not only to progressively narrow our view of the world, but also as the rational-
izing force that establishes the Leviathan as a political
power.

> The basis of authority in third-phase writing is the
> social consensus that the writer appeals to. Hence
> the modern use of language has been driven
> increasingly to define the objective reality of the
> world, on the assumption that "objective" means
> real, because it allows such a consensus, and that
> "subjective" means unreal because it does not.
> The word "subject" in English means the observer
> of the objective, and it also has the political
> meaning of an individual subordinated to the
> authority of his society or its ruler, as in "British
> subject".[22]

In this view of the order of words, humanity is cut off from
itself and, fundamentally, cut off from the basic, natural
identification humanity carries with other human beings
and with nature. Humanity loses, in Frye's sense, the freedom
that it enjoys as a community in finding words which have
been sacrificed to the dead, inert object that stands before it.
One has recourse only to abstract forms of speech such as
mathematical formulae that disclaim relationships to the
objective world in terms of a self-sustaining, tautological
system.

On the other hand, the advantages of establishing a social
consensus on the basis of this phase of writing exerts a
counterbalance to Frye's belief that human thinking ultimately must return to the poetic or the metaphorical stage.
For although the metaphorical stage of language has established a conception of God and authority, it is one that no
longer survives the entombment of the third-phase language.
One is left then in the dilemma of requiring a social consensus
on the one hand, which, on the other, denies the basis of

identity implicit in the older forms of writing. This paradox pushes Frye's position to that of the Janus-like creature who has to look outwards toward the society and the establishment of a social consensus while looking inward towards the poetic and metaphorical as a way of establishing the identity of the individual that is forever threatened in a consensual society. Here we have the basis of Frye's compromise and fall into liberalism.

The Bellman

It is at this point that Frye is pushed beyond Vico in turning to the Bible itself in the ways in which it establishes a form of writing outside of the three phases. This is reflected in Frye's view that the Bible is neither poetry nor prose, but rather some unique blend of the two which escapes the closure brought about at the end of the Vician system. Frye desperately scrambles for the ground of identity that eludes Norman O. Brown in his work *Closing Time*, however much he shares the sense in which the Vician language, as it is played out in the works of James Joyce, signals a last hurrah.

The Bible from Frye's point of view uniquely provides the grounds for what he calls "proclamations". The proclamation is seen as a combination of the metaphorical and the poetic expressed in terms of what might, in classical times, be known as rhetoric. The proclamation brings the myth down to earth as the dictum of practical reason against the two metaphors that inform the mythological, first stages of writing. The Bible stands not as history nor as poetry, and, as such, provides that blend of the two which escapes from the closure that the prison house of language holds out.

Proclamations at once are public statements made to communities, and value statements emanating from the stand of the community reflecting its primordial nature. They are at once political and spiritual. This vision of the Bible points to the balance that Frye attempts to achieve in his writings between the mythic structure of the human mind as known in the communal sense and the individual's relation to a personal God. The Bible then represents that extraordinary form of writing outside of the strict disciplines of literature or history but which provides the model in Frye's mind for the unity of the individual and the social. The Bible in a structural sense is the guide towards the metamorphosis upward of the individual's spirit. God becomes the proclaimer — the bellman.

Let the Lord have mercy on us.

William Blake, *The Bellman, Europe,* 1794

3

Mr. Golden Sun

Mr. Sun, Sun, Mr. Golden Sun,
Please shine down on me

A Children's Rhyme

Quixotes of Us All

The progress of North American society has successfully turned many, if not all, of our social interactions into various forms of cynical relations. This is the sense that Jean Baudrillard gives to late modernity under the sign of iconic power.[1] In Frye's world, this vision is one of "experience", of the fallen man, and forms one end of the spectrum of possible human situations. An end, however, that has progressively come to dominate the other end of the spectrum, the vision of "innocence." For this cynicism has even reached down into the toddler period with such universal programs as *Sesame Street,* or the rather less cynical, but boring, Canadian version, *The Polka Dot Door.*

Frye's search for innocence, nevertheless, finds in the simple and childlike the remnants of the original play in the garden before the announcement of closing time by the bellman. Children's rhymes, in part because they are non-sense, have partially slithered out from this cynical network.

As a consequence, they seem to persist as meaningful; even entering into the heads of adults many years after soothers have been exchanged for cigars.

The search for an "innocence" in the face of the experience of the closure of modern culture finds vivid portrayal in the Canadian context. Here one can juxtapose Dennis Lee's *Savage Fields*, with its grim vision of modernity, with his children's verses in *Alligator Pie, Garbage Delight* or *Jelly Belly*.[2] Lee's work underscores the quest for a moral vision rooted outside what he sees as a nihilistic structure of the social. The death of the social returns one to the child. This alternating current characterizes much of Canadian thought, as it does elements of Mexican thought. Frye shares the deep sense that the defense of culture requires the reestablishment of a moral vision. Frye will fit his vision of the New World into these bounds.

The return to childhood also sets the agenda for what is to follow in coming to terms with the basic categories that Frye uses to understand the world. More particularly, the children's rhyme, along with its pre-social status, demonstrates for Frye the fundamental characteristic of the human mind: the faculty of imagination. The child's ability to imagine is rooted in the pre-rational or in unreason as much as in the pre-social. The goal of imaginative thought becomes, by analogy, the construction from innocence of a vision of the world. As Blake would have it:

> He who mocks the Infant's Faith
> Shall be mock'd in Age & Death.
> He who shall teach the Child to Doubt
> The rotting Grave shall ne'er get out.
> He who respects the Infant's faith
> Triumphs over Hell & Death.
> The Child's Toys & the Old Man's Reasons
> Are the Fruits of the Two seasons.[3]

The cyclical nature of the seasons is the only thing that keeps Canadians from total despair, or from a total exodus from

the country. It also provides a fundamental structure to
Frye's work. To the extent that the child's toys do in the end
come together with the Old Man's reasons, Frye's world has
a unity to it. In other words, the vision of experience of the
Old Man joins the vision of innocence of the child for Frye.
This is described often in Frye's work as the apocalyptic
vision. Frye may have his 'apocalypse now' precisely because
both the vision of innocence and experience are imaginative
acts.

   The state of the imagination for contemporary individuals
is rooted in what Frye calls the vision of the great artists of
the romantic movement. Here the sense that we have fallen
away from the vision of the better world is the starting-
point. This is often attributed, as he suggests, to the loss of
the Bible's revelation, or is evidenced by any of the secular
visions that are so prominent in the history of political
theory up to the current utopian theorists.

   The imagination, as a consequence, is logically revolutionary in character, dissatisfied with what exists and forever
blowing bubbles or fantasizing about a better world. The
critical aspect of the imagination is what steers Frye away
from traditional conservative positions. It also accounts for
his identification of the structure of Marxism with the
structure of Christianity. Frye, in a political sense, is more
influenced, as we shall see, by the English revolution, and
particularly by the centrality of freedom in the liberal
tradition stemming from Locke. Being Christian on the
inside and liberal on the outside poses problems that a
Marxist who can be both Marxist on the inside and the
outside does not have. Frye will feel this tension which may
be characterized by recourse to Frye's attitude to another
great writer, Miguel de Cervantes.

   Cervantes understood that imaginative visions are not
real, and, in fact, may be characterized as "silly" at times.
Frye identifies this as a central theme in Cervantes' *Don
Quixote*. Frye suggests the childishness of some of the
adventures in *Don Quixote* must be distinguished from the
childlike qualities of innocence created by the acts of fantasy.
The point of the imagination for Cervantes and, in many

ways for Frye, is to come to grips with the loss of the golden age. As Frye suggests, Quixote's obsessions concerning chivalry are in his own way a defense of a moral code. This use of the imagination create, for Frye as well, a sense of moral realism.

The political implications of this defense of the imagination's childlike nature are more problematic. Sancho's ascension to power in the second part of *Don Quixote* continues what could be described as the ridiculousness of the whole adventure. Despite Quixote's counsel, Sancho's fate for having ruled in a moral and productive fashion is to be thrown from office, because he threatens the ruling aristocratic values. It remains to be seen whether the ticket of Sancho and Quixote would make it past the primaries even if Frye played Quixote.

It would be incorrect to ascribe Cervantes' attitude fully to Frye. There remains the question, nevertheless, whether Frye, as much as Lee, is tilting against windmills, as the expression goes. Transposed to the North American context, Frye's writings are part of the tradition which searches for moral values out of the wilderness experience which is constantly threatened by the city. This quest is the task given by Frye to the imagination in its social guise. One must ask, despite the imagination's ability to paint both the real and the unreal, whether there remains a childlike moral sense in the act of imagining. Is there a moral at the end in Michael Ondaatje's *The Collected Works of Billy the Kid?* Does the act of seeing always return to the reaffirmation of the little kid? Or, to express it as Frye does in the *Fables of Identity,* does it make Quixotes of us all.

> For this wistful sense of a golden age, lost but still possible, the child's vision which the Gospel tells us is so dangerous to lose, is something that makes Quixotes of us all, and gives our minds, too, whatever dignity they may possess.[4]

The Case for Locke

The origin of Frye's concept of the imagination is found in his struggle early in his career with William Blake. Blake is a formidable foe, for we have already seen how Blake has both the Bible and the social judgment of madness on his side. He is also one of the foremost mappers of the imagination. Blake explored the distant lands of the "unreal" with the claim that they were more real than what the "blockheads" had before them. With Blake, there was no doubt as to who the "blockheads" were: they populated the schools and universities of the land.

Thus to understand Frye's epistemology, one must look back again towards *Fearful Symmetry* and, in particular, to the opening chapters which detailed Blake's case against John Locke. In this early work, Frye introduces the basic concepts which he will later develop into his theory of the recreative imagination. The recreative imagination is a concept that is developed in the space between Blake's theories of knowledge and those of John Locke.

Blake opens his case with a proposition that Frye shares. All knowledge, action and thought stem from the human mind. This is an idealist starting-point and, as well, an ending-point. Also, under this proposition is the view that the separation of the individual from the world is characteristic of a fallen or an alienated state of humanity's consciousness. In the end, both metaphorically and epistemologically, the subject is divorced from the former oneness with the objective world. Thus, the fall or, in a more familiar sense, life on earth, creates the disjunction between the subject as primarily a knowing and perceiving being, and an objective world that stands against this subject.

Earlier, we saw how this relationship changes over time in Frye's history of the western tradition from an original unity in mythical culture to the third phase of writing characteristic of today. Beginning with Blake and continuing through the romantic period to the present day, Frye will assume that there has been a split between the subjects and the objects of the world. From his perspective, this requires the development of a "bridge" which must lead us back on the path towards an ultimate unity by re-establishing the link with the subject and object, or a unity with the self and the world. The bridge Frye establishes has its roots in the act of perception underlying the imagination. The bridge will also appear later in the chapter as depicted by Lawren Harris bringing Frye's epistemology into the social setting of the Canadian frontier. A setting that underscores the religious transcendence in Frye's view of the world.

Frye begins with the proposition, common to many variants of idealistic thought, that individuals are perceiving beings. In the formula *esse-est-percipere* — to be is to perceive — there is a sense in which the split between subjects and objects is overcome in the very act of perception. This is the child's view that the world and the body are one, and symbolizes the unity of humanity with nature found at both ends of humanity's being in time. The disjunction that enters into this harmonious world is captured in the alternate proposition, *esse-est-percipi,* to be is to be perceived. The existence of the other breaks the world in two establishing the separate realms of self and other.

Accepting, as the beginning of this split, Locke's theory that the mind is open to the world, the sensate natural environment becomes the first invader. One might say that the human world starts with the assumption of the natural world as a sensate one.

> In English literature it (the third phase of language) begins theoretically with Francis Bacon, and effectively with Locke. Here we start with a clear separation of subject and object, in which the subject exposes itself, in sense experience, to the impact of an objective world. The objective world is the order of nature; thinking or reflection follows the suggestions of sense experience, and words are the servomechanisms of reflection.[5]

Nature is sensation, and this sensation is ordered by the perceiving mind. Sensation is also likened to the funda-

mental chaotic state of nature in which the energies of life
are unformed. Hence, the human role, as a thinking perceiving being, is to bring order to this chaos through mental
activity. For Blake, this understanding is the first step
toward seeing in the act of perception the act of the poetic
genius. The more creative the perception, the more humanity realizes itself, and the more the natural world as
sensation is left behind. Locke is then overcome. Frye, on
the other hand, attempts to preserve this sensual world.
Here is how Frye expressed it, some years after *Fearful
Symmetry* in a lecture called "The Imaginative and the
Imaginary."

> In relation to the world he sees, or the environ-
> ment, the essential attitude of his mind is that of
> recognition, the ability to see things as they are,
> the clear understanding of what is, as distinct from
> what we should like it to be. This is an attitude
> often associated, sometimes correctly, with the
> reason. I should prefer to call it "sense", because it
> is a pragmatic and practical habit of mind, not
> theoretical, as reason is, and because it requires
> emotional as well as intellectual balance. It is the
> attitude with which the scientist initially faces
> nature, determined to see first of all what is there
> without allowing any other of his mental interests
> to cook the evidence.[6]

The recognition of things as they are to the senses forms one
pole of a dichotomy that Frye will develop between sensual
expression and the creative vision. This pole, like that of the
creative vision, is embedded in Frye's concept of the
imagination. Both are imaginative acts. Both are products of
the demand of the human mind to bring order to chaos.

The acceptance of the claim of the sensual world marks
Frye's acceptance of the fundamentals of Locke's case.
Although this acceptance is not without its costs, especially
in the political realm, Frye, as a literary critic, has really no
choice in the matter. The edifice that Frye constructs is

marked by the tension of the senses and reason, of the mythical and the rational, of the garden and the city. Frye must establish a relation between each term which he refers to as dialectical. In the forge of Blake's furnaces they are moulded into a single product with its claim to a higher reality.

Frye, the literary critic, must also accept the sensual for another reason. Sense impression as we can see leads to the discipline of science, and again, in this sense, moves towards the epistemological theories that Frye identifies with Locke and Bacon. The description of what is underlies what might be called the correspondence theory of truth in Frye's epistemological scheme. It is profoundly uncreative in one aspect, because the description of truth is reflective of the reality that is asserted to be in the object. Science, as a consequence, achieves objectivity through the elimination of the subject. There is no greater testament to this killing of the subject than Frye's classificatory studies: the authors disappear. The scientific world is also profoundly the acceptance of what is, turning its back on the critical and standing against the reality that is the artist's. Blake's ire against this conception of reason is unbounded, and informs his identification of the theories of Locke and Newton as the underpinning of the mediocracy which plagued his personal life, as well as being a direct challenge to his conception of the human mind as exhibiting poetic genius. For Blake, to accept this view is to accept the blind and mechanical ordering of behaviour creating the nightmarish condition of the states of war.

Although Frye is not unmindful of the demonic visions that are raised up in Blake's work and elsewhere by the total acceptance of the sensual, he cannot cut off this sensual realm for fear of losing entirely the material, natural existence of humanity in his system and his claim to science. This sensual world also is the substratum of nature upon which the technological will is at work, and from this scientific theories emanate. For Blake, one would have to be mad to believe in this world; for Frye, it is equal madness to reject it.

The Case Against Blake

The other side of the polarity between sense and the sensual world is that of the creative imagination. Again I draw upon Frye's article "the Imaginative and the Imaginary:"

> The other attitude is usually described as "creative", a somewhat hazy metaphor of religious origins, or as imaginative. This is the vision, not of what is, but of what otherwise might be done with a given situation. Along with the given world, there is or may be present an invisible model of something non-existent but possible and desirable.[7]

As Frye has stated so many times, this creative force is really at root the dynamic that transforms the rudimentary energy of the will into what we call culture and civilization. It is also the force that led Frye to characterize Blake as a creative genius rejecting the claims advanced in earlier times that Blake was mad.

Time and again, Frye will come to the defense of the writer who enters the world of language in order to save the subject engulfed by the objective order. It is the very essence of humanity's lot to be, in Frye's words, "a child of the word as well as a child of nature."[8] The very charge against the writer that he or she is subjective is precisely the saving moment against the commodification implicit in scientific language which defines the real as the objective.

Yet, if we take the polar example of Blake, his creativity may be seen as that of a visionary force placed at the far end of the spectrum of imaginative activity. To the extent that Blake's language was seen as a personal mythology, he was declared mad, and his vision labelled a disease. This fate awaited not only Blake, but any writer who strayed far from the social consensus or from nature in the creation of what Goya called the "impossible monsters" when the imagination deserts reason.[9] Blake, as we know, was saved by Frye and others for modern readers. But the price, to give the devil some due, is high.

Blake was saved, because he was talking our language all along, even if it seemed unrecognizable to the vast majority. It is true that the language was not that of social consensus: the third phase language of science. Rather, it was the language of poetry returning, as it does in Frye's mind, back to the mythical world which defines the true human community by, as he suggests, "draw(ing) a circumference around a human community, . . . not to inquire into the operations of nature."[10] Blake is reintegrated into the world, because he is a definer of a community outside of science that for Frye already exists in the visions of all poets who have the power to express it. That is, Blake is tamed, because he is linked to a shared consensus. In an odd way, Frye's Blake is civilized on the grounds of his uncreative, unoriginal, conformist elements.

Frye identifies this 'primal' language with the vision of the pastoral garden. A vision that is prevalent in the Bible, but by no means exclusively there, as he points out in the comment below linking folktales to the Bible:

> The central expression of human energy is the creative work that transforms the amorphous natural environment into the pastoral, cultivated, civilized world of human shape and meaning.[11]

The pastoral image stands for the underlying vision of the creative poet. Elsewhere, Frye describes this image in terms of the reconciliation of opposites ranging from the reintegration of humanity with nature to the sheep and the lion sharing the same quarters. It would be unfair to call this vision uncreative, or in Marx's pejorative words "rural idiocy". Yet to headlong ascribe originality to this vision in a romantic creation *ex nihilo* would also be incorrect. Frye will resort, as we shall see later, to pastoral visions to articulate the underlying reality of North American life. They form a key element in his vision. However, to the extent they indicate an acceptance in a shared mythology, they lead Frye away from Blake, the closer he gets to him.

This case against Blake forces Frye to reject the privileged place that Blake ascribes to the poetic genius. Frye, in essence, is drawing a line that begins with the imagination in its sensual form on the one hand, and ends in the unbridled imagination or vision, at the far end.

> We may therefore see the creative imagination as polarized by two opposite and complementary forces. One is sense itself, which tells us what kind of reality the imagination must found itself on, what is possible for it, and what must remain on the level of wish or fantasy. The other pole I shall call vision, the pure uninhibited wish or desire to extend human power or perception (directly or by proxy in gods or angels) without regard to its possible realization.[12]

This development of Frye's thought will lead him to reject the characterization (in the first line above) of the imagination as creative for the view that "the imagination is principally recreative:"[13] that is, the recreative imagination stands between the unbridled visionary, or Blake, and the sensual materialist, or Locke.

In fact, Frye will go further with this polarity and see in it the basis of distinction between the arts and the sciences. They circulate around, if you will, a fixed point, not following a "spindle of necessity" but rather in Frye's vocabulary a "spindle of freedom" represented by the literary critic. Frye, then, at once can stand both for and against Locke and Blake as they are in orbit around him.

Nothing New Under the Sun

The magnificent image Frye takes from Blake to describe the debate concerning the nature of the real is that of the differing conceptions of the sun. On the one hand, the sun characterized by Blake, from the Bible, as the "hallelujah chorus," and on the other hand, the sun characterized as a guinea piece of money by Locke.[14] Both characterizations are evidence of an imagination at work. Both are right for Frye; both are wrong. Nor does it help matters any by adding a third description of the sun as some bundle of elementary particles undergoing nuclear fission. They are ultimately all of a piece for Frye.

But the answer you give as to what the nature of the sun is does make a difference in terms of one's relationship to others in this world. One is reminded of the child's question in Saint Exupéry's *The Little Prince*.[15] The discussion of what the "hat" represents is used to discriminate dinner guests. It may also be used to discriminate between who is healthy and who is sick, who is right and who is wrong. As Frye points out, the closer you are to rejecting the description of the hat as the boa constrictor swallowing the elephant, in terms of the scientific-end of the spectrum, the more normal you will appear in the social setting. The further along you get towards Blake's view of the sun as the chorus of angels, the more people will decide that you have fallen into abnormality or madness. Frye draws a number of conclusions from this.

Either end of the extremes is what one might call madness. In one case, the social entirely dominates the individual, which, in the terms used earlier, would be the domination of the subject by the object. On the other hand, it is the individual isolating himself or herself from the social world in terms of a romanticized revolutionary madness, where the loss of the objective world creates the spectres of a demented imagination.

In a curious fashion, Frye's work comes very close to that of Michel Foucault in his classic treatment, *Madness and Civilization*.[16] Madness is not so much a disese, but rather a social judgment standing against individuals who are unable to present their vision in terms of the acquiescence of a social power. But Frye fails to see Foucault's sense that these visions are not natural products but rather ideological creations.

Thus, as we have seen, the imagination is not only a personal vehicle for the realization of the creative mind, but also a social category that extends from law to anarchy on the social scale. The manner in which a society will treat questions of what is the sun will tell one considerably about whether the society is conservative or revolutionary in its basic structure. Frye also shares with Foucault the sense that the imagination has primarily been posed in terms of its social use through the exercise of law. As we have seen earlier, the Bible, as an imaginative work, details the tension between the lawless state of the Garden of Eden and the fall into law and the social. In commenting on Milton's *Paradise Lost*, Frye makes this observation about Adam and Eve:

> In Milton's *Paradise Lost* Adam and Eve are sub-
> urbanites in the nude, and angels on a brief outing
> from the City of God drop in for lunch. But the
> City of God was there, along with another city in
> hell, long before the decendants of Cain started
> imitating them on earth. The corollary of this view
> was that the divine intention in regard to man was
> revealed in law and in the institutions of society,
> not in the dreams of poets.[17]

Blake's animosity to the falling of vision into the hands of social laws related very much to Nietzsche's similar opposition to the herd mentality that gives rise to mediocre and feeble wills. It is undoubtedly true that if one took a public opinion survey of what the nature of the sun was, one would receive very few answers of the hallelujah choir variety.

For Frye, the imagination forms a link between the individual and the social, or to use the language above between law and dreams. The artist, who truly understands the nature of the tool at his or her disposal, will know the individual is being drawn between two worlds of law and revolution. The understanding of this creates then the role of the educator.

The educator can transform the creative imagination and the recreative imagination into what Frye more commonly calls the "educated imagination" that can lead people from one space to the other. The educated imagination is the resultant from the tension between the artist and the scientist, or between Locke and Blake. It becomes Frye's chief social category for entering the political spectrum in an effort to avoid either submission to the law or fomenting of revolution. Thus, much of Frye's political writings will be an attempt to come to grips with this problem. His desire, on the one hand, to support a democratic, law-abiding society, and yet, on the other, his wish to fend off the madness of a social vision that relates only to itself, or the madness of an individual talking only to himself or herself, is, I believe, Frye's version of asking the "Sun to please shine down on him."

A Descriptive Catalogue of Pictures, Poetical and Historical Inventions

Frye's theory of knowledge naturally leads one to an examination of the images that inform our ways of seeing. As I have argued above, Frye understands knowledge in relation to the imagination. The imagination forms a spiral from the innocence of the child through to the experience of old age. It is also a continuum from the sensual to the visionary, from nature to the human to God. The spiral leads upward, or at least through space, to illustrate again the central metaphor of upward metamorphosis. To use a biological image, the "expanding eyes"[18] move always upward toward the sun.

I have selected, for examination, Frye's comments on three Canadian paintings. These paintings themselves reflect the nature of North America according to Frye; his commentary on them illustrates Frye's theory of knowledge.

1) Consider the Lilies

I begin with an appreciation written in 1948 by Frye of the works of David Milne.[19] In many ways, Milne represents the overall trend that Frye identifies in Canadian painting. Milne's pre-eminent concern for the problems of space is common to Canadian painting, reflecting, as Frye states, quoting Margaret Atwood, the concern for "where is here."

The spatial problem immediately translates into the existential concern for being and, in particular, the quest for a transcendence of or release from the grip of the natural world. This anxiety is reflected by the imagination's depiction of what exists in the pictures. This, for Milne, reveals the religious transcendence at the heart of the natural world.

Milne's work then turns inward, which to Frye gives evidence of the inner freedom Frye finds in the natural world. Milne in this respect represents the sensual pole in Frye's dichotomy in the very intensity with which many of his paintings focus on the here of the natural world, yet reveal a transcendence as well. Frye shares this vision of transcendence.

Although Frye draws on a number of paintings, the one that I would like to focus on is David Milne's *The Lilies* painted in 1915. It is a canvas so densely filled with lilies as to virtually destroy the long-distance perspective. It is much like a close-up photograph of a dense matting of flowers which completely obliterates any background.

The painting, as is described by Frye, draws the individual towards it. That is, the painting draws the eye towards the object in an invitation to a microscopic examination. The flowers seem under a magnifying glass, and as such stand out to the individual as the individual is drawn towards them. This leads one to see in the picture the sense of order beneath what, on first sight, would appear to be a rather random and chaotic picture. The painting also illustrates how through the imagination the distance between subject and object is reduced. *The Lilies* brings the alienated, natural world to the individual, thereby reintegrating the individual with this world.

Along with such other of Milne's paintings as *Snow On Bethlehem* or *Noah's Ark, The Lilies* shares the overall theme of the Christian experience. The lilies, as nature, hold a privileged place in Christian mythology as we know from the biblical verses about lilies not toiling. They symbolize the paradise of leisure beyond the world of use and work serving only to beautify the world and honour God. The message to the world Frye constructs is that we must cultivate our imagination to attain the insight their lack of cultivation expresses. They are effortless by nature; humans must work at it. We will meet this conception of nature throughout Frye's work where the artistic rendering of what exists reveals the paradise of the biblical garden.

The Milne painting is significant in another respect in that it captures very precisely the sense in which all reality, as perceived, is a type of surrealism. That is, the Milne painting stands out, in Frye's words, "as though the whole picture were floating in the air detached from its rectangular frame"[20]. The Milne paintings appear to be suggesting that even at the level of the senses and of nature, the apprehension by the human mind is the upward metamorphosis towards the higher reality. In the 1948 commentary, it is expressed this way:

> Few if any contemporary painters, in or outside Canada, convey better than he does the sense of painting as an emancipation of visual experience, as a training of the intelligence to see the world in a spirit of leisure and urbanity.[21]

This upward metamorphosis is only able to occur in a leisured environment which, as we shall see, draws Frye's word "re-creation" towards contemporary society's view of "recreation" or what we do in our leisure-time. Recreation is predominantly the sign of an advanced urban society which again is why Milne's paintings, in Frye's 1948 commentary, curiously foretell the direction in which Frye's thought would steadfastly move.

2) Across the River and Out of the Trees[22]

The concern to bring the individual to terms with the environment and through this to terms with himself or herself Frye also discovers in many of the works of the Group of Seven. In fact, the Group of Seven has come to be seen as ' typical' of the Canadian painter's reaction to the

North American experience at the first part of this century. The complete commercialization of the Group of Seven, and especially paintings of "The Lonely Pine" variety, has destroyed much of the freshness and originality of the pictures. It has also spawned poetic anthologies entitled *The Blasted Pine* in self-defense. Most Canadians experience an almost uniform revulsion at seeing yet another example of the Group of Seven anywhere, especially in dental offices.

Whether this judgment is fair or not as an evaluation of the Group, I would ask the reader to mentally conjure up any one of these pictures, but preferably one from Tom Thomson. I would suggest Thomson's 1915 picture entitled *The Northern River* which depicts a small river wending its way through the forest until it disappears at the back of the picture. Again, an early quote from Frye, this time from 1940 in an article entitled "Canadian and Colonial Painting", is very useful for setting the parameters of Frye's approach.

> What is essential in Thomson is the imaginative instability, the emotional unrest and dissatisfaction one feels about a country which has not been lived in: the tension between the mind and a surrounding not integrated with it.[23]

The description echoes Frye's earlier view that the relation humanity has to the natural world is predominantly a fallen one, thereby setting the objective world in tension with the imaginative mind. This reveals a sense of the early New World as beginning in the alienation of the individual from the natural environment, a view which especially dominates the period of exploration. It is a depiction of Canadian culture that will recur in Frye's later comments on Canada.

The results of this alienation refer back to Frye's conception that the imagination reaches outside the self. The imagination leads the individual to a space beyond where he or she is. The Canadian reality, at the time of Thomson's *Northern River*, is not fully able to project the visionary prophecy of a William Blake. It must remain content with pointing towards the promised land which is "across the river and out of the trees." Such a view is clear in the following passage from Frye's 1965 "Conclusion to a *Literary History of Canada*."

> The sense of probing into the distance, of fixing the eyes on the skyline, is something that Canadian sensibility has inherited from the *voyageurs*. It comes into Canadian painting a good deal, in Thomson whose focus is so often farthest back in the picture, where a river or gorge in the hills twists elusively out of sight, in Emily Carr whose vision is always, in the title of a compatriot's book of poems, "deeper into the forest".[24]

So much of the Canadian reality is then bound up in the phrase of the "next year country": one always looks to the future for the reconciliation with the environment. This also describes perfectly for Frye the elements of the visionary artist who similarly is always looking beyond what exists for a vision of a New World.

3) The Bridge

Both the Milne perspective and the Thomson perspective are drawn together in Frye's commentary on a book of paintings by Lawren Harris.[25] In particular, Frye focusses on Harris' painting, *The Bridge*. *The Bridge* can, as a symbol, quite obviously represent many things, and Frye is not reluctant to have it serve a number of his purposes. I will comment on two points that Frye notes in introducing the paintings.

First, Frye sees the painting as bridging the perspectives of subject and object. If Milne's paintings can represent a form of subjectivity that excludes the object in drawing the object towards the subject, and if Thomson can represent the object devoid of a relationship to the subject, then Harris is firmly planted in both camps in Frye's mind. *The Bridge,* unlike *The Lilies,* maintains a sense of distance from the viewer. Yet, it is a sense of distance that is not lost in taking the eye to a far-away place which is always beyond

Lawren Harris, *The Bridge,* 1937

one, but which, as with *The Northern River,* may be exactly the same as where you came from. Anyone who has paddled down a river knows the feeling of an end which is always in sight yet always receding. *The Bridge* from its resting spot on both perspectives alters the sense of space upwards. This is similar to many of Frye's images that move the eye towards the higher reality that, in Harris' picture, abounds in sunlight.

Second, the Harris painting also points out how directly Frye sees the relationship between the works of art and society, and in particular how this painting is a bridge between Harris' faith and the civilizing moment in the Canadian experience. To quote from Frye's 1969 article on Harris, reproduced in *The Bush Garden*:

> The first and most important of his "bridges" is the bridge between the artist and his society. He is missionary as well as explorer: not a missionary

who wants to destroy all faith that differs from his own, but a missionary who wants to make his own faith real to others. Just as new country cannot become a civilization without explorers and pioneers going out into the loneliness of a deserted land, so no social imagination can develop except through those who have followed their own vision beyond its inevitable loneliness to its final resting place in the tradition of art.[26]

The vision of the Harris painting is, in the end, a communal vision that shares the childlike simplicity of the individual-God relationship. To employ an older, romantic vocabulary, the painting rests on the sense of the sublime which places the individual in awe before the transcendental reality of a higher vision. The individual is reduced to the level of the child by the terror of natural world, but a controlled terror under the eye of God.

I will be following Frye on his own bridge towards a vision of the social. On the one hand, this will lead us to Frye's view of Canadian society where I will take the bridge not only in its metaphorical sense, but also as the invasion of the technological will in the transformation of nature into a higher spiritual reality for Frye. This will set out the tension between the pastoral simplicity of the lilies, and the extension of the technological empire to bridge the distances in the development of Canadian society. The second perspective will be that of the relationship of this imagintion to the development of a social theory. I have called this the liberal imagination in Frye's thought, which I now turn to examine.

4

The Liberal Imagination

Have leisure and know that I am God.

Psalm, no 46[1]

Northrop Frye's case for liberalism must be seen in the context of the boundaries set by the critiques of liberalism on the part of two Canadians, C.B. Macpherson and George Grant. Both Macpherson and Grant bring to their critiques a concern for the North American experience. Macpherson's critique stems, in part, from early studies of the social credit movement in Alberta that lead him to reject liberalism's claim to maximize the potential of each individual. Grant, on the other hand, sets forth the involvement of North American liberal society in the technological world. He stresses the sense of the individual's communal nature cut off by technology. For Grant, social existence produces a 'lament' that forces the individual to find solace in the religious world.

Contemporary liberalism is, as a consequence, attacked both for its claim to honour individuals, and for its claim to found a community. Thomas Hobbes remarked in the introduction to *Leviathan* that there is a tension between liberty and authority: "it is hard to pass between the points of both unwounded."[2] This, nevertheless, is what Frye will attempt.

C.B. Macpherson has demonstrated in his *The Political Theory of Possessive Individualism*,[3] that the root of the liberal theory of government extends back to the writings of Thomas Hobbes and John Locke. Macpherson captured the dynamic of the English revolution in the claims to freedom made by the possessive individual. Unfortunately, this revolution also brought along the dispossessed who were deemed to be part of society when it came to assuring law and order, and, therefore, willing signatories to the social contract. Yet the majority of individuals were manifestly excluded when it came to the division of the spoils of the property system. Property establishes its grip over individuals through the relational power of class divisions. As Macpherson has related in his later work *The Life and Times of Liberal Democracy*,[4] an exorcist, democracy, was called in to rid the liberal model of this tension, thereby creating what we know today as liberal democracy.

Not even the strongest advocates of liberal democracy in the nineteenth century did so without some anxiety over the consequences of taking seriously the equality postulate in the democratic model. In the writings of a reformer like John Stuart Mill, the tension between wanting to include everyone in the social contract and yet fearing for his own cultural existence rendered many of his works almost schizophrenic. Mill offered a number of solutions ranging from the plural vote for the university-educated (a notion that today not even one's undergraduates greet with any level of enthusiasm) to, perhaps, the more lasting of Mill's attempts to get out of this dilemma, his advocacy of the advancement of education. Macpherson, having shared the North American reality with its somewhat greater equality of condition, continues to remain sceptical that the exclusionary rights of the property relationship will ever be overcome in a liberal model.

Conservative thinkers have made considerable headway against the liberal view in pointing to the debasement of culture attendant upon the democratic franchise, however much this culture might, in the end, be, as Marx suggests, merely the ideas of the ruling class. In particular, the force of

Grant's critique joins Nietzsche's scathing views on the nihilism implicit in the will to power of the herd mentality. Grant extends the analysis of the will to power to see in the American empire a technological dynamo that furthers the nihilism of late capitalist society. Canadian liberalism's collapse into continentalism is just one sign of the debasement of a culture that has abandoned the principles of justice for the extension of the technical power of the market. George Grant finally joins the tradition of religious thinkers exiting the debate, leaving society floundering in the technological world of power on the one hand, while the individual turns towards God on the other.

Frye's liberalism must be located in this intellectual debate. It is, on the one hand, an attempt to save the cultural aspects of society without the fall into conservatism. On the other hand, Frye wishes to reconstitute the basis of a liberal society away from the possessive individual's property right towards the common property of language and literature. The contract moves from the socio-political realm where it is burdened, as so many of the critics of liberalism have suggested, by the inequality of original condition, to the realm of communication. Liberalism rests, then, on sharing ideas with each citizen through Mill's solution of the educational contract which Frye endorses. This brings together the concern for education and freedom. As Frye suggests in *The Critical Path*, "The educational contract is the area of free thought and discussion at the centre of John Stuart Mill's view of liberty."[5]

It is with this foundation that Frye will answer the questions as to the origin of values, and what constitutes the ethical norms of a good social order. In the end, this liberal order will founder upon the very principles on which it is built. The prophecy of Frye's vision returns again to the authority of a class-divided, technological vision that orders the energy field in the aspiration towards freedom. It is a vision that is consumed by the contradictory foundations of liberalism. However, in the effort to solve the crisis of social identity, it gives rise to the entrance of a new player to govern the rules of the game. No longer the statesman, the philosopher-King, nor for that matter the poet, but rather the detached spectator, the literary critic appears as the Aristotelian citizen most fit "to govern and to be ruled."

Spengler's Fall

The basis of liberal theory is the assertion that individuals, by nature, are both free and equal. This original equality is usually ascribed to a state prior to society, or government, called the state of nature. Following traditional liberal models, the state of nature begins as a form of golden age or paradise where individuals are believed, either through fact or fiction, to have lived harmoniously with each other. This will reappear later in Frye's conception of the "good friend." However desirable this state might have been, 'things conspired', to refer to Jean-Jacques Rousseau's version of how we got out of this paradise, to render the state of nature more like the state of war. Frye reads the states of nature and the states of war as various mythologies that have been created to buttress liberal ideology. While the vocabulary is different from that of the expulsion from the Garden of Eden, the change in the state of nature of liberal thought can be likened to Frye's concern with the mythology of the fall.

This mythology is traced, as we know, by Frye in numerous authors. In fact, in this respect, Frye's work is encyclopaedic. Frye has read and commented upon virtually every major writer. The usual fate is that they become grist for his mill used solely to define the mythological structure of the human mind. However, this is not solely the case with Oswald Spengler, whom Frye defended when Spengler was not popular. This stretches back to the earliest points in Frye's career, and recurs periodically in his writings.

For my purposes, Spengler will provide the assumptions underlying Frye's view, within a social setting, of the fall into "civilization." Spengler opens *The Decline of the West* with a series of rhetorical questions that go to the heart of the assumptions that Frye will make in his philosophy. Spengler assumes that all questions of history are founded upon archetypes which he identifies in the opening pages of *The*

Decline with the general sense of biography. Frye will not limit himself to the biographic reference. The sense in which all existence in time is cyclical is a major premise for Frye. Both individuals, and society are structured upon birth, life, death and re-birth. In the twentieth century, following Spengler, we are in a state of decline, and a serious critic of society will document this decline.

Spengler's case rests upon his fundamental distinction between culture and civilization, and the role that the artist and critic play in this system. Spengler describes it thus in *The Decline of the West:*

> Civilization is the inevitable destiny of the Culture, and in this principle we obtain the viewpoint from which the deepest and gravest problems of historical morphology become capable of solution. Civilizations are the most external and artificial states of which a species of developed humanity is capable. They are a conclusion, the thing-become succeeding the thing-becoming, death following life . . .[6]

Culture is seen as the indigenous product of individuals exercising their talents as myth makers. This is the individual alive in the original state of nature prior to the fall into the state of war. This also reflects the importance of understanding the local culture, and, in our case, the culture of North America as the source of the energy which will be used in the formation of civilization.

Local cultures, and here I would say that for Frye this includes the Canadian culture, span what uncharitably, yet correctly, may be called "vegetable consciousness." That is, they are products that are alive, have very great seasonal values, are readily consumed, but in some sense have no lasting value. This sense of culture will inform the comments on Frye's understanding in the North American context of the movement from culture to technological civilization.

Spengler also gives us an insight into how one moves

from culture to civilization through the works of critics and artists. From what I regard as a very revealing quote in Spengler, we gain a direct insight into the various ways Frye's conception of civilization harbours within its core a commitment to a technological world-view. Quoting Spengler:

> No one has seriously considered the possibility that arts may have an allotted span of life and may be attached as forms of self-expression to particular regions and particular types of mankind, and that therefore the total history of an art may be merely an additive compilation of separate developments, of special arts, with no bond of union save the name and some details of craft-technique.[7]

Cultures are, from Spengler's point of view, spatially oriented and time bound. A similar view is expressed by Harold Innis. In one sense, then, the uniqueness of a culture to an outsider cannot be 'carried away'. In contrast, by its very nature, civilization, in this view, transcends individual cultures because it is premised on death, or completion of the various forms of culture. Civilization exists, then, in time in a manner that culture does not, while civilizations are beyond space while cultures are in space. Civilizations are universal, or imperialistic in Spengler's words; cultures are particular, and so it goes. The transition, nevertheless, occurs as Spengler has pointed out, through the development of craft-techniques, or, to use a different vocabulary, through the development of technology itself. Frye recognizes this influence in his 1967 lectures entitled *The Modern Century*.

> Spengler is often dismissed as 'fatalistic' today, but his paralleling of our historical situation with earlier periods, especially that of the Roman Empire, and his point that our technology could be part of a decline as easily as it could be part of an advance, are conceptions that we all accept now,

whether we realize it or not, as something which is
inseparably part of our perspective.[8]

To express this in a different fashion, the energy of nature
which gives rise to the culture is structured by the forms
brought to it by the civilizing individual. The civilizing
moment of a society is precisely when these forms are
recognized and catalogued by the artist and critic. The
moment shares the same space as the technological impulse
that governs science for Frye.

The dilemma that Hobbes saw between the horns of
freedom and authority is now shifted by Frye to the authority that flows from the cataloguing of craft-technique by
the cultural critic. This represents a fundamental shift in the
liberal paradigm away from the authority structure based
solely upon law and upon prophetic authority. Here the
New World consciousness and the New World vision come
together in the reinforcement of the technology at the base
of western progress. While this technology has emancipated
the New World from the traditions of classical thought, it
has spelled the closure of European civilization. In Spengler's
words, this is called "the world-embracing spatial energy of
modern technics."[9] For Frye, this is expressed in *The Great
Code* where he marks the movement to technique or inner
authority of a discipline as a replacement for prophetic
authority. The argument also supports the case for liberal
pluralism.

> In the modern world, therefore, what corresponds
> to prophetic authority is the growth of what we
> called earlier a cultural pluralism, where, for
> example, a scientist or historian or artist may find
> that his subject has its own inner authority, that he
> makes discoveries within it that may conflict with
> social concern, and that he owes a loyalty to that
> authority even in the face of social opposition.[10]

Frye sees himself as a mapper of civilization, which I believe
he is attempting to be. He is creating the authority of a new

discipline, criticism, which, in the North American context, will render the prophetic writer's vision secondary to the disciplinary bounds of scientific, or technological, law.

Life is magically, or rather technically, turned into forms, or death, for Frye. He treats the products of cultures as artifacts. A similar perspective was adopted by Roland Barthes, the French literary critic who in his middle works dealt with myths. Each of them has pursued the Aristotelian urge for classification. In the physical sciences, taxonomy no longer is at the forefront of the disciplines. Yet Frye, in viewing literary criticism as a young science, claims the necessity of indulging in this cataloguing for which he is extraordinarily adept.

The taxonomy, nevertheless, has its useful side. In an upward metamorphosis, it sweeps all particulars towards universals. Spengler's comment that "the Morphology of world history becomes inevitably a universal symbolism"[11] captures exactly the project of Frye's studies. This sets up Frye's case for the development of values as universals, as well as his claim that liberal society has a social contract based upon universal consent. It is a form of classic, tacit consent precisely because we all use the same symbols. And if you do not know the symbols, then, of course, we have the educator to teach you.

"Mansions in Eternity": The Case for Kant

Frye's comments on Spengler's work, as well as those we have seen earlier on the Bible, come together in Frye's identification of the structure of existence as a universal, cyclical phenomenon. Indeed, one can go further to suggest, as Frye does in *The Return of Eden,* that the central existential concern of humanity is for the recovery of a lost identity, hence the cyclical nature of existence, the "lost and found" common to us all.

> . . . the central myth of mankind is the myth of lost identity: the goal of all reason, courage and vision is the regaining of identity. The recovery of identity

> is not the feeling that I am myself and not another,
> but the realization that there is only one man, one
> mind, and one world, and that all walls of partition
> have been broken down forever.[12]

The centrality of the myth leads Frye's thought to the form
of romanticism that he identifies with the recapturing of the
golden age. As I will show, this is a form of the apocalyptic
vision premised on the *a priori* synthetic ideal of the unity of
opposites, or to express it as Frye normally does, the view
that the lion and the lamb will lay down together. It is also a
return to Immanuel Kant.

On one level, this is very similar to what Kant expresses
in his *Idea for a Universal History*, particularly in the ninth
proposition where Kant sets out the ideal of "a universal
history of the world in accordance with a plan of nature
aimed at a perfect civil union of mankind."[13] In another
work "The End of All Things", Kant provides an insight into
the reason why he pursues this universal ideal. To contem-
plate the opposite proposition, in Kant's words, brings one
to "the brink of an abyss, and for him who sinks into it, no
return is possible."[14]

In one of the most perceptive comments on the twentieth
century, however little Kant intended it to be so, he then
proceeds to document what would happen if one did, indeed,
look into the abyss. He compares such a life to that of an inn
where one is constantly being replaced, to a penitentiary, to
a lunatic asylum and finally to a cloaca or sewer which, as
Kant suggests, turns the garden away from the "many
trees . . . with magnificent fruit, the residuum of which,
however, disappeared into an imperceptible effluvium after
their enjoyment."[15] Despite the fact that natural swamps are
good for the garden, Kant would have no more of this than
Frye would, and returns to the more reassuring vision of the
universal harmony of humanity. Yet the negative vision
provided by Kant is very similar to the "dung-eating madman
Ezekiel" of Blake's work which, Frye points out, is quite
often the end of the prophetic vision.[16] Frye's reluctance to
pursue this prophetic aspect has been noted earlier, and

marks one of the boundaries in Frye's thought when confronted with the existential problems of the wilderness.

This turning away from the 'abyss' has been noted by the American philosopher Michael Weinstein. His perceptive work, *The Wilderness and The City*,[17] documents the failure of the American will, at the turn of the twentieth century, to face questions of moral identity. The American response under the impulse of the idea of progress tends towards the nihilistic will to power and is manifested in the violence of the imperial civilization. This phenomenon is clearly found as well in Canada, but the response is found in the turn to religion, a disposition which George Grant and Frye ultimately share. I will show later how Frye uses this difference to argue for Canadianizing the United States.

The reluctance to confront fully existential questions also has a profound effect on the types of social contracts that Frye believes are appropriate in the attempt to recapture a sense of identity threatened by the sense of the abyss. For Frye, the "cloacal" image is profoundly disturbing because it marks so drastically the history of western civilization. It is a manifestation in his mind of the separation of individuals from nature and the reduction of humanity to effluence. Thus the social contract must close itself off from the conception of law and order dominated by the social standards of sanity and reason. Not wishing to stare down the problem, to use modern vocabulary, of the existential situation, Frye must turn back again to the pre-biblical sense of the unity of humanity with the world. Here is how he expresses it, again, from *The Great Code:*

> The reason for this degeneration of the world ruler is one that takes us back to the two forms of social contract that we saw arising out of the pagan and Biblical cultures. The Classical social contract is the one that we see in the trial scene at the end of Aeschylus' *Oresteia*. It is a vision of justice and equity in which man, nature, and gods are all included. The gods ratify it, and if they were not there we should have nothing but the purely

automatic reactions of nature represented by the Furies, the agents of the natural force of *nemesis*, to keep a balance in human affairs. In the Biblical contract, as we saw, nature is not an immediate participant: the contract is between God and his people, and if the people are as loyal to it as God is, the nature around them will be transformed into a quite different world.[18]

Frye's preference for the classical contract in the above, is marked, for it captures the sense of unity among humanity, nature and God, excluding, if you will, the metaphoric royalism so central to the expression of the biblical social contract.

The bad news is that this contract does not exist now and, undoubtedly, never really existed in the past. However, the good news, for Frye, is that it does not matter. The whole point of an ideal is precisely that it does not exist, no more than do Kant's *a priori* propositions concerning the good political contract that honours freedom, independence, and equality. Frye is more on the romantic side of things preferring a pastoral image that he returns to often in his discussion of Canada. For both Kant and Frye, there is the possibility that one's reward will indeed be in heaven or, to use the Blake expression that forms the title of this subsection, one may have a "mansion in eternity."

Ultimately, the made-up nature of both beginnings and endings of Frye's mythological structure culminate in the loss of any conception of time and space outside an apocalyptic vision, an experience that few of us wish to test The thorough-going routing of experience which Kant attempted is not open to Frye. While Kant and Frye both share the view that the individual is in everyday life predominantly irrational and governed by desires, still, in the Kantian system reason predominates over mythology. Frye's attempt to get behind Kant is to prove that Kant is the "largest human brain," yet one who failed to see his own mythological origins. Nevertheless, the Kantian project, by specifying mansions in heaven, provides us with the direction or standard to guide our actions. This is the sense in which, I believe, one should take Frye's essay on the social context of literary criticism entitled *The Critical Path*. We now join Frye on the stairway to heaven.

The Critical Path

Frye's 'critical path' leads him directly into the liberal political model. It makes of Frye an establishment figure, linking him with the predominantly liberal attitudes that have characterized Canadian politics, and uniting him with liberal political theory in general. It also strikes to the core of Frye's philosophical position. The path towards Macpherson's rejection of the power relations of capitalist society is blocked by the movement of the political for Frye to the realm of mythic consciousness. The inequality of the human condition is embedded in the need for an 'upward metamorphosis.' Social change then becomes secondary to the mental change of a "larger human brain." The path to Grant is also blocked. Grant's sense of deprival of the self in the technological world translates poorly into Frye's sense of lost identity. Again, mythic consciousness is all around us and, like the fish in water, we have failed, for Frye, to recognize it. For Grant, the waters have been deliberately polluted, and we, as a consequence, have suffered the injury of this deprival; it is not a matter of forgetting.

The basic irrationality, or mythic nature, of the liberal position as a social theory, becomes the background (most often not acknowledged) to the individual's quest for identity. Frye claims that the premise of lost identity structures the nature of all social myths. One is left with the view that Frye's ideological commitments to liberalism supercede the sense that social myths are premised far more on a concern for creating a sense of justice for the individual in the future, not looking for 'lost virginity.' The 'convenient' forgetting of the social allows Frye to regress to the presocial or the family, where the end of all myths comes down to the sense of oneness felt in the fraternal view of the selfhood of humanity. Here, of course, there is no need for the distinction in Frye's vocabulary between the individual and the other, individual consciousness as mythic consciousness, as universal consciousness, as bliss.

Frye, nevertheless, proceeds on the premise that identity has been lost and with it comes the necessity for the creation of the social: a social that is dedicated to the recapturing of the lost identity and, therefore, is under the sign of what Frye calls the myths of concern. Concern is asserted to be in Frye's works an existential category which will govern the manner in which societies structure themselves. Myths of concern relate back to Frye's sense of the western tradition as grappling with the fall. Hence, the corpus of all the arts really form, in his mind, the content of concern. But more fundamental, it is the mapping of the liberal personality over the cracks in the social edifice. The myths of concern in the end become the mirror reflection of the liberal imagination. In common vocabulary, it is putting on a happy face.

Nestled within the myth of concern are three other mythologies that underlie Frye's conception of the liberal imagination. They are the myths of religion, of freedom, and of education. Taken together, Frye asserts these myths create culture in the large sense, and are designed to address the "anxiety" stemming from the identity crisis.

I begin first with an examination of the myth of concern. As the reader might expect, the myth of concern in its highest form is exactly the same as the poetic, religious vision of the William Blakes of the world and the Bible. That is, as Frye states in *The Critical Path,* "Poets have always been the children of concern."[19] Poets have lived with the anxiety that the loss of identity produces. This is true of their work. At the highest level of such activity, such as in Blake's vision, they have recreated the primal sense of identity for Frye.

The child might well ask what is wrong with that. The slightly wiser and older Frye of *The Critical Path* gives us a number of answers. As we have seen earlier, Frye is reluctant to follow the visionary imagination; a reluctance that is even greater when it comes to social theory itself. Frye shares a distinction raised by Karl Popper between open and closed societies. Religious societies, or societies governed by poets, move towards closure. In Frye's mind, this stands against the notion of being "good friends." It is in the very nature of a vision of identity to define who we are and, in doing so, to exclude who we are not. Thus, myths of concern are products of the local space, of the *polis,* to use the vocabulary of classical political thought. And if one follows the logic of the earliest political philosophers and, in particular, in the opening book of Plato's *Republic,* these myths define our friends and enemies. If this undoubtedly reflects an element of the cold war fears typical of the period in which much of Frye's writing has occured, that is part of it, but only part, for it leads back to the dilemma again posed by the tension between Locke and Blake over the role of the poet in a social setting.

The case against the poet reappears quite strongly in Frye's *The Critical Path*, and it centres on the age-old problem of how to tell if the poet is truthful. Here is how Frye states it:

> A more disturbing question is whether there can ever be truth of concern that is not in some degree falsehood of correspondence; whether myth must lie, and whether there can be any piety, to whatever church or state, without some kind of pious fraud.[20]

Noble lies and all, we are back to the classic distrust of the poet expressed by Plato. To express this as Frye does in the old faculty psychology, the individual is by nature irrational, hence a myth-maker. Thus to trust the myths fully is to trust the passions. The passions notoriously do not correspond to the Lockean consciousness or the truth of correspondence.

Taken together, the myths of concern as religion are predominantly what Frye identifies as the basis of conservative, political thought in the western tradition. Organic societies are dominated by mythic consciousness where a person's identity is fused in the overall sense of community. The dominance in North America of the American dream and of American patriotism shows just how conservative a society it is in terms of its mythological unity and how threatening this society is for Frye when linked with technological consciousness. Having gone through an individualist revolution, a conservative society is no longer possible, in Frye's mind, except through the throwing up of false gods and the suppression of individualism so typical of the New Conservatism in the United States.

Frye's rejection of the poets turns him back to the core of the Lockean case which is to be developed in the myth of freedom which Frye sees as a controlling myth. Freedom is the tolerance of a plurality of myths of concern. Interestingly enough, the myth of freedom does not stand against myths of concern as a direct opposite but is portrayed itself as being a myth of concern.

> The myth of freedom is part of the myth of concern,
> but is a part that stresses the importance of the
> non-mythical elements in culture, of the truths
> and realities that are studied rather than created,
> provided by nature rather than by a social vision.[21]

The passage is revealing in a number of ways. Frye is resetting the basis of truth and myth in a form of the *Critique of Pure Reason* which displaces the role of the philosopher: rather than Nietzsche's musical Socrates, we have a poetic Aristotle. In this way, Frye is giving the western tradition his distinctive twist essentially through the privileged position of the critic. The anthropological problem of identity is solved 'by the epistemology of the studied individual.'

This passage is also remarkable in its location of freedom outside of society. Frye is here recreating one of the essential, political concepts of western society in nonpolitical terms. Similarly, society is asked to find its vision outside of the social. One of the reasons for Frye's apolitical and asocial stands is given in his attribution of freedom to nature itself. This is the origin of Frye's liberalism and takes one back to the world of John Locke. The John Locke here is not that of the *Essay on Human Understanding* but that of the *Two Treatises of Government*. Man is pictured in the state of nature as free, equal and peaceable, or at least until "vain Ambition, and *amor sceleratus habendi*, evil Concupiscence, had corrupted Men's minds,"[22] thus setting the individual on the road to the state of war. Whereupon the individual entered the social contract under the control of reason, and was to leave behind visionary and poetic ways.

If we follow Frye's words on freedom, they lead us back again to the world of Milton where, as we have seen before, freedom is the burden that God has placed upon us. In Milton's sense, there is a fusion of the myth of freedom with the myth of concern.

> In Milton's view, the prophetic writer has recovered the poet's original role of teaching the myth of concern; and because of the revolutionary impact of the prophetic tradition, the message of concern is identical with the message of freedom. Liberty is what the will of God intends for man, but it is not anything that man naturally wants, his nature being perverted.[23]

Yet even if we grant Frye's view of Milton, the fusion of revolution and tradition of Milton's period is no longer open to contemporary man. Milton's energy has been altered from the will of God to the technological will to power. The myth of freedom, like the myth of religion, is predicated on a world that has disappeared. Frye's thought, in many ways, oscillates between these two disappearing poles of freedom and religion or, to use the vocabulary at the beginning of this chapter, between the concerns of Grant and of Macpherson. In blunter terms, Frye's position is gored by both these 'horns.' The contradictions in nature between war and peace are absorbed into Frye's view of the individual and the social, compromising his thought. This cross-fire is set up by the predominance of another myth that claims to satisfy all concerns, and that is the myth of progress. Frye's thought is pushed toward the ground he hopes to avoid, that of technology as the mediation of liberalism.

Wheel Within Wheel

I see the Four-fold Man, The Humanity in deadly
    sleep
And its fallen Emanation, The Spectre & its cruel
    Shadow.
I see the Past, Present & Future existing all at once
Before me. O Divine Spirit, sustain me on thy
    wings,
That I may awake Albion from his long & cold
    repose;
For Bacon & Newton, sheath'd in dismal steel,
    their terrors hang
Like iron scourges over Albion: Reasonings like
    vast Serpents
Infold around my limbs, bruising my minute ar-
    ticulations.

I turn my eyes to the Schools & Universities of
    Europe
And there behold the Loom of Locke, whose Woof
    rages dire,
Wash'd by the Water-wheels of Newton: black the
    cloth
In heavy wreathes folds over every Nation: cruel
    Works
Of many Wheels I view, wheel without wheel, with
    cogs tyrannic
Moving by compulsion each other, not as those in
    Eden, which,
Wheel within Wheel, in freedom revolve in har-
    mony & peace.

William Blake, Jerusalem[24]

For the twentieth century, the wheels have, indeed, "cogs
tyrannic." The harmony and peace of the Eden myth is far
off, and it is far off because the modern individual has taken,
in Frye's view, the critical path to be the path of progress.

The shifting of revolutionary consciousness from God to the myth of progress is continually doomed to failure precisely because it can never address the problem of identity.

> ... progress is a social projection of the individual's sense of the passing of time. But the individual, as such, is not progressing to anything except his own death.[25]

The attempt to conquer 'death' or overcome the bounds of time has its roots in North America in the development of the perspective of science and, in particular, through the production of technology with its stress upon movement and space. This is the sense of progress which seeks to address the problem of identity but for Frye creates alienation of the individual, not only from the self, but from objects in the world. Yet the central roles of science, technology and progress underscore the difficulty that Frye has in excluding entirely the myth of progress as a response to the social dilemma. I have shown earlier Frye's dependence on the view that life is energy, a view shared in the Hobbesian world by market-oriented individuals pursuing their powers in a capitalist society. Frye's experience in the North American context has certainly taught him that alienation may be reduced through the extension of the communications empire which, after all, is a way of shrinking time in space.

Indeed, the dilemma creates, for Frye, a new view that society is divided into three sectors: the political, the economic and what he refers to as the leisure society. There is no doubt that Frye's commitment to the benefits of capitalism requires that progress be maintained in the economic realm. The danger of the economy, as he points out, is not so much that one accepts the claims made by the advertising industry, but rather that one becomes dependent on the version of reality that underlies these claims. Here is where the myth of progress becomes pernicious in structuring the question of identity.

We have also seen the difficulty Frye has in locating the existential concerns in the political realm. The experience of the rule of law, be it in the biblical myth or for that matter in the conservative view of society, sufficiently scares Frye because of its threat to individualism. This leaves Frye with a third alternative: to develop a social mythology based upon a conception of leisure.

Frye's case for the leisure world joins his case for the importance of the educated imagination as the basis of a liberal, pluralistic model. In fact, we see that the development of technology, in Blake's vision, does not necessarily preclude the harmony of the wheels within wheels of Eden. One might say all they need is more grease. For if the development of technology does not preclude the return to Eden, it then must be able to open up the possibility of chaining the technological drive to the development of the essence of liberalism. This essence reappears as the basis of the educational revolution in liberalism.

> Thus the technological revolution is becoming more and more an educational rather than industrial phenomena.[26]

Thus if we follow the logic of Frye's technology, we are led to a new version of the social contract which is dependent upon not an industrial revolution, but rather on the educational/technological revolution, a vision reaching as far back as J.S. Mill's work. The "education contract" is seen, by Frye, as replacing the central role of the traditional, social contract of liberal theory — a replacement made on the basis of the claim to superior reality of the arts and sciences.

> It is clear that such a society (or social contract) has only an interim and emergency authority. Behind the transient appearance of society are the permanent realities of the arts and sciences which education leads us to. It is obvious, therefore, that the social contract has to be supplemented by an educational contract.[27]

In moving to an educational contract rather than the more standard contract based on a claim to economic or political factors, Frye is able to adjust his view of the nature of liberalism and, in particular, the relationship to social class. Education, following one of the traditional readings of Plato, can only take place in the absence of coercion whether this be political force or traditional work. Thus for Frye, as for other thinkers such as Josef Pieper, the non-political is at the basis of civilization, the nonpolitical, in the sense of the social class with leisure to engage in activity outside the working realm.

The Marxian concern for the wage/labour relation is relegated to the realm of progress. In Frye's sense, a working culture by definition always remains uncivilized. We are back again to the schools and universities of Europe, not to mention the New World. But this leisure world is, nevertheless, exactly the world that corresponds to the kingdom of peaceable ends of the mansions in eternity.

> Fraternity is perhaps the ideal that the leisure structure has to contribute to society. A society of students, scholars, and artists is a society of neighbours, in the genuinely religious sense of that word. That is, our neighbour is not, or not necessarily, the person in the same national or ethnical or class group with ourselves, but may be 'a good Samaritan' or person to whom we are linked by deeper bonds than nationality or racism or class solidarity can any longer provide. These are bonds of intellect and imagination as well as love and good will.[28]

Leisure: A Spectator's Sport

The image that I have created of Frye's liberalism may be summed up in the vision of an educational contract based upon a sense of freedom that is outside of society. The social contract in a shorthand fashion is no longer political or economic except when forced to be, at which time one

invokes the "emergency authority clause." Another way of
expressing this is that politics, if it has any role at all in Frye's
vision, plays that of referee between competing claims. This
is the role ascribed to the democratic element in the liberal
democratic mixture. Here might be what one could call the
critique of practical reason from *The Critical Path*:

> The only practical solution seems to be the one hit
> on by democracy when it was trying to pare the
> claws of Christian temporal power. This is to
> accept, as part of a permanent tension between
> concern and freedom, a plurality of myths of
> concern, in which the state assumes the respon-
> sibility for keeping the peace among them.[29]

We are, in many ways now, back at the beginning of Frye's
career with the *Anatomy of Criticism*. Frye began his seminal
work with the injunction against carrying questions of taste
into questions of values. The average man on the street
could have a view as to what constitutes good literature, but
it should not be confused with the scientific criticism raised
by the detached objective critic. In the third of Kant's
critiques, the *Critique of Judgment,* questions of taste or, for
that matter, literature are set upon a universal basis although
without the claim to certain truth made for the earlier
critiques. The point is that Frye follows the same direction.
He tries to establish values on the basis of distance from the
competing biased claims of the individuals with their
particular myths of concern. I have shown how Frye attempts
to make his educational contract a contract without politics
grounded in the sense of the natural world or in the sense of
the crisis of identity. Yet to postulate a social system without
a sense of political power, or political actors, even as an
ideal, is hardly acceptable.

One, of course, could not leave Frye at this point for
there has to be an answer, and, indeed, there is. The ref-
ereeing of social visions, the sport that goes on in the leisure
society, falls, as I have indicated earlier, to the role of the
literary critic. In Max Weber's sense, we have now the

chosen vocation of the literary critic. For the literary critic deals with the world at a fundamental level denied to the prophet, wiseman or counsellor, as this reference to Frye's *Divisions on a Ground* suggests:

> The prophet becomes less of an ecstatic and more of an adviser or counsellor, and the wise man comes to be thought of as having a potential of utterance called forth by certain occasions. Both are drawn towards the present, and away from the past and future. And as wisdom and prophecy approach each other, it becomes clear that there is a point where they meet and become the same thing, the point where there is no longer any wise man or any prophet, but simply the word itself, a power of speech articulating itself independently of the speaker's ego.[30]

Here we have come full circle. The appearance of words that speak themselves through the critic. Here is Frye's liberal imagination as a vision.

"Have leisure and know that I am God."

5

Vegetable Consciousness

The question of identity is primarily a cultural and imaginative question, and there is always something vegetable about the imagination, something sharply limited in range.

The Bush Garden

Preludium

"Dark Virgin", said the hairy youth, "thy father stern, abhorr'd,
Rivets my tenfold chains while still on high my spirit soars;
Sometimes an eagle screaming in the sky, sometimes a lion
Stalking upon the mountains, & sometimes a whale, I lash
The raging fathomless abyss; anon a serpent folding
Around the pillars of Urthona, and round thy dark limbs
On the Canadian wilds I fold; . . . "

America: A Prophecy[1]

Frye's vision of North America takes us back to Blake's picture of the Canadian wilds and Orc's struggle with the powers of nature. These powers give rise, as Frye has written in *The Secular Scripture,* to an "improbable, desiring, erotic and violent world,"[2] which must be absorbed by the modern consciousness. The absorption of this "dream world" is the civilizing moment, but it is a moment, as I have shown, that hides within itself the alienation of identity. As Frye suggests in the opening quotation to this chapter, the question of identity resolves itself into both cultural and imaginative aspects. Another way of expressing this is to say that the question of identity rests on humanity's natural existence in time and space. In particular, the relationship established by consciousness with nature, or the vegetable world, forms a theoretical groundwork to the recreation of identity.

In the beginning, mythic consciousness does not separate the subject from the object, the individual from nature, or time from space. For Frye, and for Innis, European cultures capture their sense of values from a dependency on time. Men are bound to their communities through the sharing of values across cultural and national boundaries. This is ultimately the religious sensibility. The North American experience, by contrast, has been that of the empire with its predominant emphasis on spatial questions. The conquering of space is by the 'screaming eagle,' the 'stalking lion,' or the abyss is confronted by submerging into the dark kingdom of the whale. Thus Frye, in his "Conclusion to a *Literary History of Canada*," detects in the 'famous struggle' for Canadian identity a shift of the question away from the subjective question of identity to the spatial question of location.

> It seems to me that Canadian sensibility has been profoundly disturbed, not so much by our famous problem of identity, important as that is, as by a series of paradoxes in what confronts that identity. It is less perplexed by the question "Who am I?" than by some such riddle as "Where is here?"[3]

The shift of the question of identity to one of space over time sets out Frye's project as that of establishing a space-binding mythic consciousness. The goal of this consciousness will be to recreate the unity with nature, the unity that is itself entwined with the technological imperative that confronts North America. This is a vision of a society that attempts to bring a spatial closure to the myths of concern. This tension informs Frye's vision of North American and, in particular, his sense of the Canadian identity. It takes up Orc's challenge to couple with Urthona to produce the new generation, but a new generation that has tamed the eagle, lion and whale. Frye traces the serpent's grasp that re-establishes the fall into the Canadian wilderness which makes sexual relations safe and beavers of us all. I return now to the state of nature.

The Taciturn Beaver[4]

Let us go back to the beginning, excluding, of course, any sense of a beginning that our native peoples might have. The beginning, in this case, as pictured below, is a map drawn by the European Herman Moll who was born in Holland, then emigrated to England in the 1680's and remained there until his death in 1732. Moll was an artist cartographer and, similar to many members of his trade, had never visited the places he depicted. This, nevertheless, did not stop him from depicting *The Cataract of Niagara*.

Although one could have chosen a number of sites, Niagara is especially useful because it captures both the American and the Canadian experience. Despite many similarities in these experiences, the experiences of Niagara will indeed prove to be quite different. Frye points out that the route to Niagara Falls, in the case of the Atlantic traveller to the United States, begins immediately after crossing the ocean as one enters New England. Here the grip of Albion over its progeny, the New Albion, is never fully loosened. As Blake would have it, "The Guardian Prince of Albion burns in his nightly tent: Sullen fires across the Atlantic glow to America's shore,/Piercing the souls of

Herman Moll, *The Cataract of Niagara,* circa 1690

warlike men who rise in silent night."[5] The American experience never severs the tie with Europe returning, as I shall show later, in the primacy of the sense of time over space brought about by the technological will to empire.

To enter Canada, on the other hand, is, as Frye suggests, to be swallowed up by an alien and forbidding continent as one travels up the St. Lawrence River and through the Great Lakes. Thus, from the beginning, the very spatial dimensions of the two countries yield different experiences to the explorer. The friendly reception that greets the visitor to the United States is in stark contrast to the voyage to the "heart of darkness" through a hostile, natural environment. The Canadian experience is one of struggle with space reflected in the timelessness of the mythology of entering the whale.

The Moll depiction has a theoretical use as well, for it portrays clearly the fact that all states of nature are constructions. Frye refers to the genera as varieties of "literary

Utopias."[6] I would prefer to see them as varieties of political visions reflecting the artistic imagination at work. The Moll depiction of *The Cataract of Niagara* is useful in another respect in that it unveils a conception of nature as energy and industry. The notation at the bottom of the map reads, in part, as follows:

> A view of ye Industry of ye Beavers of Canada in making Dams to stop ye Course of a Rivulet, in order to form a great Lake about wch. they build their Habitations.

Although Frye would not necessarily agree with this as a depiction of the state of nature, it captures Frye's insistence upon human nature as energy, and the fact that this energy is portrayed in a technological fashion. The beavers, upon close inspection, resemble rather nasty human beings, certainly giving the indication of the possibility that their harmony may yet break out into a state of war or animosity. In Robert Kroetsch's phrase those beavers have the potential to become "exploding porcupines." Yet, as they are depicted, their technological activities lead, as the Moll quotation suggests, to the sense of habitation through the transformation of nature. Although, as beavers, they need not fear alienating themselves from the natural world and, similarly, have rather little use for speech: 'energy without alienation.'

Frye, in his very perceptive "Conclusion to a *Literary History of Canada,*" expresses what I believe to be a similar notion in the following way.

> Culture is born in leisure and an awareness of standards, and pioneer conditions tend to make energetic and uncritical work an end in itself, to preach a gospel of social unconsciousness, which lingers long after the pioneer condition has disappeared. The impressive achievements of such a society are likely to be technological. It is in the inarticulate part of communication, railways, and

bridges and canals and highways, that Canada, one
of whose symbols is the taciturn beaver, has shown
its real strength.[7]

The taciturn beaver then stands as a symbol for the beginnings of the conquering of the Canadian space, but also
stands for a registering of the technological will inside of the
development of the identity that Frye traces from the
primordial state through to the modern century. I will
propose other pictures of beavers, rather less industrious
ones however, as Frye's conception of the end-point of the
pastoral myth. I will refer later, in particular, to the paintings
of the American Edward Hicks. I think the contrast between
the Hicks and Moll paintings underscores how deeply Frye's
pastoral images are ideological commitments.

Mementos of the Fall: Mosquitoes[8]

Frye's conception of Canada has been strongly influenced
by the poetry of E.J. Pratt. We have met earlier Pratt's
Towards the Last Spike which begins by documenting the attack
on nature made by the engineer Van Horne and the politician
Macdonald in the development of the Canadian railways.
Pratt, among Canadian poets, stands foremost in Frye's
mind as creating the mythic consciousness that binds space
together. He might be described as the railway builder of the
poetic set. He also documents a sense of nature which is
radically different from much of what Frye finds in American writing. Pratt's concern with the conquest of nature
stems not so much from an urge for conquering physical
nature (represented by the construction of a railway across
the continent) but rather from the sense that nature is
hostile because it is "cruel and meaningless" and must,
therefore, be overcome if humanity's potential is to be
fulfilled. Time and again in Frye's path-breaking studies of
Canadian poetry for the *University of Toronto Quarterly,* he
returns to the sense in which nature in Canadian poetry is
depicted as sinister and menacing in an existential sense, and

that the Canadian soul has been formed by this struggle with the hostile environment.

> To sum up. Canadian poetry is at its best a poetry of incubus and *cauchemar*, the source of which is the unusually exposed contact of the poet with nature which Canada provides. Nature is seen by the poet, first as unconsciousness, then as a kind of existence which is cruel and meaningless, then as the source of the cruelty and subconscious stampedings within the human mind.[9]

This sense gives rise to one of the most famous of Frye's images, that of the garrison mentality. Here the state of nature has been turned into a state of war, not through the break-down of human relations, but rather by the confrontations of the human mind with its environment. The black-flies and mosquitoes drive Canadians from the bush garden and are an ever present reminder of our fallen condition. They also create the closed spaces; forms of North American polis which come to stand for the country. And similar to the polis, the garrison generates a society with the moral and social values, as Frye suggests, of the propertied middle class. The garrison communities are held together solely by means of the communication line between each of the communities and by the sense of a struggle to find a shared space. They share a common sense of mission to conquer the intervening space in order to be heard. Frye calls this development the centrifugal movement where identity is sought outside itself and in the art of communication. A similar sense I have shown earlier in the paintings of The Group of Seven.

The American experience stands in marked contrast to the Canadian, in Frye's mind. Frye points out the well known differences attendant upon the lack of a revolution in the Canadian historical past and the influence that revolution has had on America. But, more fundamentally, the American experience in conquering the continent has failed to escape the dictates of the focus on time. The concern for time is a concern for values to counter the technological consciousness that renders the American experience nihilistic. The obliteration of space through technology destroys all local culture; hence destroying the ground for values sending the American consciousness to abstractions that transcend the spatial dimension. Frye ascribes this to the development in the eighteenth century of European rationalism in the United States, again a revolution that did not appear in the more religious Canadian consciousness. The dependency of the Canadian nation relative to the United States created, as well, the marginal existence in space for Canada with the attendant objective to live with the technological will of the United States without full dependency. This is depicted in the American way of life in the concern for progress and the linking of technology to what Frye calls mechanical rather than organic or existential conditions prevalent in Canada.

> The United States found its identity in the eighteenth century, . . . This in turn developed a rational attitude to the continuity of life in time, and this attitude seems to me the central principle of the American way of life. The best image for it is perhaps that of the express train. It is a conception of progress, but of progress defined by mechanical rather than organic metaphors . . .[10]

There are any number of paintings which capture this sense of 'progress.' One artist among many, Robert Whale, made his living from such pictures. Two, in particular, are rather interesting. They both can be brought to mind by imagining *The Cataract of Niagara* now devoid of beavers but with a train running across the foreground. Whale actually painted two pictures with the same setting, one entitled *The Canadian Southern Railroad at Niagara* and the other entitled *Whole Panoramic View of Niagara Falls with the Michigan Central Railway Train.* Other than Whale's hedging his bets as to which country would come out on top, it is interesting to note in these pictures that one train is entitled "The American Express"

while the other is entitled "Baggage Express". The joining
of nature and technology that Whale depicts is very close to
what Frye sees as the alliance that made America great while
the Canadians were left back at the station still entrapped in
the service industry. Niagara Falls' current role as a tourist
attraction and a dump site for pollutants is, perhaps, not too
far from Frye's view of the eighteenth century or the aftermath
of Whale's view.

The differences between the Canadian and the American
perspective come down to the fact that Canadians have had
to face the existential dilemmas of their country in a fashion
different from that of the United States. The technological
will of the United States drives out all considerations of
nature. The lyric in Joni Mitchell's song, they have "paved
paradise," is not far from Frye's view of the matter. The
attack on nature also stands for the violence prevalent in
American life, especially that celebrated in the "wild west."
The poetic depiction of this violence in Michael Ondaatje's
The Collected Works of Billy the Kid details the collapse of the
value structure of the American folk-hero into technological
nihilism. The violence in subduing nature is displaced onto
the social structure where violence is exercised against
humans under the sway of the will to power. Human identity
is submerged in the unnatural quest for dominion by destruction alone. This leaves little room, as I have suggested,
for Quixote. The level of iconic power of the six-gun leads
quite 'naturally' to that of larger technology of the MIRVs.
At this point, American culture has itself been displaced for
the internationalism that underpins technology which
destroys all local culture and individual identity.

> But when we look at the United States itself, we
> can see that there is nothing American in the de-
> basing of standards: that is simply human inertia,
> and such inertia destroys everything distinctive in
> American life equally with Canada.[11]

The creative energy of freedom for Frye becomes dissipated
in the imperial civilization.

The Canadian, on the other hand, is forced to come to an accommodation with nature through the use of technology which, Frye will claim later on, can present us with a view of humanized technology. The garrison becomes, in Frye's words, the "revolutionary garrison" in the movement from the struggle for survival in a cultural and a physical sense towards a national society. The usual refrain that the Canadian West was more civilized owing to the presence of the Mounted Police is drawn out by Frye to support the argument of mutual accord between humanity and nature. Canada saw its identity in the contract that governed both the taming of individuals' wild desires and the frontier's rough physical nature. Far from being a one-person show, the attack was the beginning of a corporate state capitalism in which it was bad business policy to shoot your source of labour or have them shoot each other. It also is symbolized in the frailty to this day of the accord with nature. The mosquitoes have been held only temporarily at bay, not obliterated, and are quite able to recapture the country or, at the very least, cut the lines of communication. The Canadian identity has its roots in the consciousness of these 'furies' outside of the individual's control.

The coming of age of North America is marked, as a consequence, within the bounds of these visions: an accommodation with nature and the overcoming of nature. They are two extremes along the axis of technology. They are captured, for Frye, in two paintings from the nineteenth century.

Cabbages and Kingdoms

I have suggested at the heart of Frye's vision of the New World a tension in the concern for identity between the claims of nature, on the one hand, and the individual, on the other. These claims are mediated by technology. The experience of the New World, whether from the Canadian or the American perspective, begins in the technological response to space. Frye, when he contemplates this technology, draws close to other Canadian theorists who have mapped,

Erastus Salisbury Field, *Historical Monument of the American Republic*, 1876

what Arthur Kroker calls *Technology and the Canadian Mind* in his study of Innis, Grant and McLuhan.[12] Thus, this technological will should be seen as a continuum from Frye's sense of the culture as a vegetable state on the one hand, to the sense of civilization or empire on the other; or the world of cabbages and kingdoms, to use the Alice in Wonderland rhyme.

The dualism of vision also serves as the core of Frye's "Conclusion to a *Literary History of Canada.*" Here Frye provides the documentation from the American experience of the vegetable or Eden myth on the one hand, and the myth of empire on the other. Frye takes two American painters to illustrate his theme. The first, Edward Hicks, we have met before in the discussion of the Niagara Cataract. The second painter is Erastus Salisbury Field. I will deal with the paintings in turn.

The Field painting, as can be seen is an extraordinary work painted in 1876 for the centennial of the American revolution. It captures the full-blown technological world view of the Americas. Not only is the picture colossal, but the detail points out how strongly Field captures the sense of empire associated with the Americans overcoming European culture. The spires are classical in style which serve to raise the sense of the history of the American civil war depicted on them to permanent marks of high culture. The sense of grandeur and importance is equal to anything from the past. The monument is also symbolically an overcoming of the tower of Babel where all is in harmony under the aegis of the sense of progress of the empire. Particularly interesting are the railroad bridges that run along at the tops of the spires. The crowning glory as it were. Frye comments on this painting as follows.

> It is a prophetic vision of the skyscraper cities of the future, of the tremendous technological will to power of our time and the civilization it has built, a civilization now gradually imposing a uniformity of culture and habits of life all over the globe.[13]

The very real difference between this picture and that of one of the Canadian garrisons at about the same time is striking. It reinforces Frye's view that the American culture suffers from the alienation of progress to a degree that threatens the very cultural and artistic life of the country. Nature has absolutely no place in this Field painting, symbolizing for Frye the ultimate disappearance of nature through technology. Frye notes that this vision also appears in more modern writers such as the American author Thomas Pynchon. Pynchon is a cataloguer of the disappearance of nature in favour of a technological sky-God subjugating Mother Earth, to use Frye's language. The technological will to power is also prominently in the Field painting, a will in time rather than space. Space has been totally subdued in the dedication of the painting as an historical monument. The sense of value has been destroyed, yet the iconic power of the vision yields the message of the domination of technique.

The second painting that Frye uses to represent the other end of the imaginative dichotomy is one by Edward Hicks. Frye has selected *The Peaceable Kingdom,* painted around 1830. I have chosen, instead, to reproduce an earlier Hicks painting of 1825 entitled *The Falls of Niagara.* The religious symbolism of this picture is strikingly clear. Note the serpent in the foreground and the small human figure on the right of the picture in the upward metamorphosis pose of hands held high. The beaver seems to be contentedly munching away on a stick watched serenely by the stag to the left. And, as if we did not need it, Hicks has provided us with colour-commentary straight from the vocabulary of the sublime where "This overwhelming work of awful Time . . . That should bid us kneel, and Times great God adore."

The Hicks painting underscores how deeply Frye's own sense of the vegetable consciousness ultimately returns to the realm of the Garden of Eden. The Niagara Falls of Herman Moll or Edward Whale is here virtually unrecognizable. The Hicks painting transforms a vision outside experience into apocalyptic time. Frye's comments on the similar painting, *The Peaceable Kingdom*, illustrate his deep commitment to the theological vision which is at odds with his own analysis of the tradition in Canadian poetry in its attempt to overcome nature.

> It is a pictorial emblem of what Grove's narrator was trying to find under the surface of America: the reconciliation of man with man, and of man with nature . . . This mood is closer to the haunting vision of a serenity that is both human and natural which we have been struggling to identify in the Canadian tradition. If we had to characterize a distinctive emphasis in that tradition, we might call it a quest for the peaceable kingdom.[14]

Here is the heart of Frye's ideological vision in his attempt through recourse to the peaceable kingdom to exit from the nightmare of the technological vision represented by the American Republic. The vision also marks Frye's abandon-

Edward Hicks, *The Falls of Niagara,* 1825

ment of the local cultures which are, in his words, "sharply limited in range" for the wider compass of belief. The "astonished eye" has seen the vision of the Lord, and needs to see no more. The vision, like Ezekiel's chariot, travels beyond space and time.

Exploding Porcupines

At the heart of all social mythology lies what may be called, because it is usually called, a pastoral myth, the vision of social ideal ... The nostalgia for a world of peace and protection, with a spontaneous response to the nature around it, with a leisure and composure not to be found today, is particularly strong in Canada.[15]

The assumption of a pastoral myth at the base of all social visions is the key assumption sustaining the edifice of Frye's

social and political writings. It is key not only to his attempt
to turn away from the completed technological vision, but it
is at the foundation of the conception of the leisure society.
But, in the end, it is an ideological structure. The 'taciturn
beavers' must confront the 'exploding porcupines' as we
enter Kroetsch's 'badlands'.

The 'badlands' reflect the fact that society cannot turn its
back upon the technological vision any more than it can
return to the Niagara Falls of the Hicks painting. Ultimately, Frye is forced to move his conception of social vision
towards a "humanized technology." The shift occurs most
prominently in the "Second Conclusion to a Literary History of Canada." Indeed, it must come about in Frye's
thought precisely because the development of the North
American consciousness has been intimately tied up with
the communications established by the technological extension of the garrisons across the country. The beavers,
after all, were engineers.

> Meanwhile, Canada, traditionally so diffident, in-
> troverted, past-and-future fixated, incoherent,
> inarticulate, proceeding by hunch and feeling,
> seems to be taking on, at least culturally, an inner
> composure and integration of outlook, even some
> buoyancy and confidence. The most obvious
> reasons for this are technological. The airplane
> and the television set, in particular, have brought a
> physical simultaneity into the country that has
> greatly modified the older, and perhaps still under-
> lying, blazed-trail and canoe mentality.[16]

The underlying reality of the North American experience is
still that of the explorer extending the lines of communication following Innis' fur trade, in Frye's words, the 'blazed-
trail and canoe mentality.' Thus, there is a "buoyancy", in
Frye's mind, to technology which leads one to see, in such
things as television, the form of communication that has a
genuinely humanizing aspect.

There are two very important conclusions that one might draw from this line of argument. The first is that Frye's case, in the end, comes down to an argument for improved technology. In Frye's words, we need a more imaginative way of seeing things that retains the social vision of the pastoral myth, yet honours the technological underpinnings of this myth in the energy of the taciturn beavers. From my perspective, this is an argument for "improved binoculars."

The second, from Frye's vantage point, is that the Canadian nation has avoided being an empire and, as a consequence, has avoided the technological end-point of the Erastus Salisbury Field vision. Indeed, Frye goes on further to suggest that the American prophecy, in the end, is more informed as a Canadian prophecy.

Canadianizing the United States

Perhaps it is not too presumptuous to say, although few non-Canadian readers would understand what was meant, that the American way of life is slowly becoming Canadianized.[17]

The take-over of the United States by Canada has been going on for some time. It started from the day the first immigrants reached the continent, although the awareness of the fact is not much greater now as then. The development has, nevertheless, been recorded according to Frye in the mythology of origins and the quest for adventure, or more directly as he suggests in Frederick Philip Grove's *A Search for America* which carries as its subtitle, conveniently enough, "The Odyssey of an Immigrant."

Grove claimed to write the book in 1893-94, scholarship sets the book closer to 1920, with Frye picking out the timeless character of the book. The plot is rather simple; the central character is a penniless upper class European who moves to the New World to restore his previous wealth and then to reclaim past glories. Life not being like that he receives a New World education in terms of the American economic imperative and then achieves an inner freedom upon finding the Promised Land (in the contentment of the soul); a form of conversion of the Odyssey to the New Testament. Another way of stating this following Stanley McMullin's introduction to the work is to see it as part of the debate over the future of the Americas "by those who favoured the agrarian life against those who felt that the new convenant could best be achieved through the advances of an industrial society."[18] This is a restaging of the tension between the pastoral image and the technological imperative which is worked out in Grove's mythology through the spiritual adventure of Philip Branden. Both Grove and Frye side with the pastoral viewing the technological will as in the end a form of closure on the soul.

Branden's encounter with the economic structure of the time underscores deeply the deprival in the pursuit of technological progress. It is a deprival that is found throughout the class structure of the United States, and only is countered in the story by the marginal figures such as the hermit that precipitates Branden's spiritual change.

The book contains as a plot as well, the tension between life in the United States and life in Canada, with Canada taking on the role of the marginal culture. This is emphasized in the last chapter when Grove waxing at his best 'sermon on the mount' style declares:

> The masses were fed, in Europe, from the cities; the masses were fed, in America, from the country. Blessed is the nation that remains rural in this respect, for it will inherit the world.[19]

The industrial revolution in the United States was turning the rural areas into agri-business under the control of city lawyers and bankers as the concluding vignettes of the book detail. This led Grove in a footnote, which one could take as autobiographical reference, to conclude that the ideal of America had been abandoned in the United States signalling for him "one reason why I became and remained a Canadian."[20] Another way to state this is back to the 'vegetable consciousness' of Canada with its concern for life.

If Frye was inclined to share Grove's vision at the turn of the century, Frye's later comments on the United States only serve to underscore the rapidly worsening situation of the Republic. The obliteration of the "peaceable kingdom" in the United States in the intervening period signals the triumph of technique which precipitated the moral crisis in American thought. Frye describes this crisis as the relegation of physical nature to outer space, symbolized by the American space program and space age technology.

Nevertheless, eternal banishment of nature is impossible in Frye's world for the relation of humanity to nature always resides in mythic consciousness. Back to the poets especially in Canada to E.J. Pratt's "The Truant"[21] where the technological sky-God is rejected by the truant humanity. Or, we have seen earlier, back to the Canadian discourse on technology in the works of Havelock, Innis, Grant, McLuhan or Frye. This turn to humanizing the technological imperative is also found in the United States. Frye's contemporaries in literary criticism, such as Geoffrey Hartman, Harold Bloom and Kenneth Burke, share the sense that values must be re-established in the wake of the nihilism of the post-Nietzschean world. Frye's response to them is that this project has been the Canadian reality and that the "solutions" they seek will be that of humanized technology stamped 'made in Canada.'

6

Improved Binoculars[1]

One of the derivations proposed for the word Canada is a Portuguese phrase meaning 'nobody here'. The etymology of the word Utopia is very similar, and perhaps the real Canada is an ideal with nobody in it. The Canada to which we really do owe loyalty is the Canada that we have failed to create.

The Modern Century[1]

Let us begin this next chapter with Frye's comment that the country of Canada is unoccupied and probably does not exist. It may be there for the making or, perhaps more precisely, the taking. Canada, whose existence is still cloudy, may then spring to life – although perhaps only for a short time. What better way to create *ex nihilio* than by the coupling of two venerable Canadian institutions, the Canadian Broadcasting Corporation and Northrop Frye, in the series of radio lectures entitled *The Educated Imagination*.

The CBC is drawn together with Frye in an attempt to overcome the diaspora afflicted on humanity or at least on North Americans. We know from Frye's stress upon the universality of the apocalyptic vision, that this creation will be done with a bang, a bang which must end in the over-coming of differences between peoples. Logically then, the search for humanity begins in the skies. In particular, with the spires of the technological empires where one should look for the overcoming of the confusion of tongues. And, indeed, the Tower of Babel might sustain itself as an overall image of Frye's project. Here is how he expresses it in *The Educated Imagination.*

> The particular myth that's been organizing this talk . . . is the story of the Tower of Babel in the Bible. The civilization we live in at present is a gigantic technological structure, a skyscraper almost high enough to reach the moon. It looks like a single world-wide effort, but it's really a deadlock of rivalries; it looks very impressive, except that is has no genuine human dignity. For all its wonderful machinery, we know it's really a crazy ramshackled building, and at any time it may crash around our ears. What the myth tells us is that the Tower of Babel is a work of human imagination, that its main elements are words, and that what will make it collapse is a confusion of tongues. All had originally one language, the myth says. That language is not English or Russian or Chinese or any common ancestor, if there was one. It is the language of human nature . . .[3]

So let us mount the contemporary Towers. There are lots of them about: the World Trade Centre, the Sears Tower, the crucifix atop of Mont-Royal and the one that Northrop Frye and I share, the so-called Canadian National Tower in Toronto. We may be able to see who does live in Canada and what language they speak.

Pictures From the Tower

The C.N. Tower is an especially apt symbol of Frye's main themes for it is both an upward metamorphosis and a vehicle for communication. The C.N. Tower is simultaneously the highest and lowest point in Toronto: the highest structure built upon the lowest point of ground. Symbolically this is very rich as Frye's criticism shows. It is also the folly of a city talking to itself. To the north of the tower, there are the backyards and TV rooms of the Wagschals and the Chambers—painters we will meet in a moment. To the south lie the Great Lakes and the American empire. One could imagine Alex Colville on the beach below the tower. Here the 'improved binoculars' look across towards the American empire from 'whence cometh news of the world.' Finally, from on top of the tower, we will be able to catch a glimpse of Northrop Frye.

1. June Noon

Perhaps the Colville picture, as much as any, summarizes the quest for the religious transcendentalism that inspires so much of Frye's thought. This search has brought a critical moment to understanding our society both in the technological dimensions that render the universal language of human nature that Frye hopes for, and the pastoral myth that structures Frye's view of the New World. Yet, the search for an ethical imperative based upon the religious vision seems to leave the world behind.

For Frye, along with Colville's man, there is a curious forgetting of the nude woman in the tent in their search for an identity. The man is standing on the beach with binoculars. He is looking out upon the nihilistic landscape of the perfectly still ocean. Here the eye passes beyond the 'astonished eyes' of Hicks, or the 'expanding eyes' of the lilies seeking the sun. The binoculars introduce the technological eye with its powerful but ever narrowing focus. The sun at high noon is hardly a factor in the stare of the man out on nothingness. The erotic and desiring world of the body is rejected, captured in the downward glance of the woman. Colville's work is at once a devastating critique of the emptiness of the ethical world and a frightful insight into the power beyond the magnified gaze. The energy of the man becomes the laser-like force of the piercing vision — a vision that captures the alienation of man and woman beyond friendship, intimacy, sex or life: the sterility of the fall of the modern Adam and Eve.

Alex Colville, *June Noon*, 1963

It may be that, for Frye, all visions are reducible in the end to that of the biblical story. And it may be that the language of human nature is only intelligible at the end. But the Colville painting places a serious obstacle in front of Frye. The 'upward metamorphosis,' symbolically that of the tent harbouring 'being,' goes nowhere as the eye is taken out to the emptiness of the sea. Here revelation becomes pure alienated energy: no noise, no movement, no God.

The tension between energy as 'unalienated' or creative, and energy as 'alienated' under the stasis of the rules of technique explodes Frye's vision. The Colville painting along with the others to follow rip open the "natural world" underlying this vision. In the end, Frye abandons his concern for a poetic or artistic vision that can structure and order existence. The aesthetic, imaginative vision is rejected in favour of the universality of the literary critic. Yet, this path leads to the similar universality of the technological sky-scraper which destroys the ability of a culture to regenerate itself. Frye's politics remain deeply compromised; in a positive way praising the local nature of culture against the international homogeneity of civilization, while simultaneously negating its vision.

Frye's emphasis on the imagination in the life of the country is important. Yet, an imagination that is, in the end, no more than a recreative educative tool brunts the force of the very poetry and literature that it has sustained. There comes a time, which has surely been reached by most poets and painters today, when they have left Frye's criticism behind to sustain themselves on their own merits. It is true that they are still classified, many times, by the systematic nature of Frye's literary criticism. But as contributors to the political and social myths of the country, the poets and painters are now going their own way. It is not that one would expect the resurrection to come about solely through the creative vision. Vision divorced from the political becomes solely a useful thing to hang in art galleries.

However, the combination of political force with an imaginative vision may provide the humanism that Frye was searching for, but which he ultimately fails to find. In a society that increasingly pays homage to the image to structure its political power, one ought to look to image-makers like Colville. For, after all, the drama in the Bible comes, in part, from the competition by the image-makers.

2. Sunday Morning

The Jack Chambers picture is one that will be familiar to any parent on the weekend who, anxious for the leisure of the peaceable kingdom of one's bedroom, sends the children from this fertile garden to the historical monument of the American empire, the television set. And, indeed, on the television screen, there appears an Austrian yodeler carrying a flag. In this the children were lucky, for the vast majority of programs on a Sunday morning in North America are revivalist programs of the evangelical ministries. However, in the Chambers painting the stars in the window suggest very clearly the Christian iconography that domi-

Jack Chambers, *Sunday Morning*, 1969-70

nates the inner soul of the North American viewing audience
– at least according to Chambers. The outside is the winter
wonderland that incarcerates the population, creating in
Tom Wolfe's wonderful phrase, "other places of exile, other
Canadas of the soul."[4] The language here is universal, it is
religious; but what of the children?

The unity of the technological vision and the religious
vision is often laid aside by the view that the inner soul is
ultimately immune from the probes of the hyper-kinetic
society. Frye's own juxtaposing of the pastoral image
against the technological nightmare is evidence of this. Yet
the Chambers work, like Colville's, strips the religious
experience to the level of iconic power which holds the
children firmly in its grip. Indeed, the children are "freed"
by the post-natural consciousness of the television to see the
flag-waving Austrian under the paralyzing presence of the
Christian image. The invasion of the soul is completed by

the Christmas tree in the window, drawing the reader to the conclusion that on this birthday Christ's will be a still-born.

The children have been captured by the apocalyptic bang that started the modern world. No longer the background radiation of modern physics' cosmology, but the everywhere present radiation of the promotional culture that fills the air waves. The universal language of humanity has silenced the children; the communicative explosion replaces speech. Even the light takes second place to the television which overcomes both light and darkness in the laser-like pulsation of energy into the twenty second attention span of modern society. The emptiness of the room merely serves to highlight the abandonment of the children to the world of images through TV, mirrors, windows and reflections which are all around. On top of it all the TV is portable ready to go anywhere in the Volkswagen parked in the driveway, itself at the time, rivalling Christ for popularity.

The privileging of the religious moment in the struggle with the existential condition of individuals in the world is a similarity in what are otherwise the disparate themes of McLuhan, Grant, Innis and Frye. The call for ethics based on this 'religion,' as above the visions of the artists, may create the ideal of humanity, but it can, in the end, only further serve to marginalize the concern for values by creating a hyper-cynicism: the religious artifact as cynical commodity. The Colville and Chambers paintings underscore the silent nihilism inside the quest for values. We remain within the Nietzschean vision broken only by the hyper-realism of the paintings themselves.

3. The Backyard

The most powerful of the images employed by Frye is that of the Garden of Eden. Throughout this study, I have shown how Frye has recourse to the pastoral image as the saving grace that counters the development of the fall. Yet the middle classes too have their gardens, their times of peace, their times of leisure. The *Backyard*, by Marian Wagschal, presents a rather different image of the struggle

Marian Wagschal, *Backyard*
by permission of the Confederation Centre Art Gallery
and Museum of Prince Edward Island

with nature that informs so much of the early part of Canadian painting and poetry. Here the struggle has been won. Eve is still waiting for the snake or the apple or something in the background, despite the heavily laden tree full of pears. The children, doll-like in the carriage and contentedly on the grass, epitomize cherubic, suburban angels. They have been moved from the Chambers painting into the Wagschal work. Father sits barefoot and pudgy in his lawn chair, with his vacant stare. Temptation lies in front of him on the glass table. It is cake that looks like a green frog. But father is beyond temptation. Man's good friend is at leisure just off the chemically treated lawn.

For what Wagschal points out is, of course, nothing unknown to Northrop Frye, which is to say that the modern images of the pastoral convention can hardly escape the technological ordering of our cities. Some backyards are, of course, better than others, and, of course, many have no backyards at all. This particular backyard obviously only exists in Wagschal's mind and my neighbourhood, in the fashion not too different from the backyards of Edward Hicks' *The Falls at Niagara*. But the Wagschal painting has what is denied to the idyllic, pastoral images: the focus on life in the local culture. Wagschal presents, in the end, the vegetable consciousness of the here-and-now, and not the international style in which Frye's pastoral images finally result. The vines that line the garden in their very lushness form an impenetrable prison. There will be no prince, as in the child's story of Briar Rose, to break through the vines to end this sleep. However much they are "having a wonderful day", they remain isolated and unhappy. We are in the world of Magic Realism without any magicians.

4. Through a Glass Darkly

What about Northrop Frye? Here I will relate a story that Frye quite often recounts. Frye was born in Sherbrooke, Quebec but spent much of his time being educated in Moncton, New Brunswick. In 1929, he entered Victoria College at the University of Toronto as an undergraduate student. This required his commuting from New Brunswick to Ontario which, at that time, the late 20's and early 30's, required one to make extensive use of the trains. As the journey was long, part of it had to be made in darkness. As anyone who has had the opportunity of travelling by night in the train knows, the environment is soon obliterated by the reflection of oneself outside the train window. Frye's journey from Moncton to Toronto yielded the image of himself which, in a way, is the point of the search for identity that informs so much of Frye's writing.

It is perhaps fitting that this study which began with Blake's *America: A Prophecy*, under the clouds in stormy conditions of the vegetable world of generation, should end with an image of Frye: Frye of the mountains, lakes, rivers, and plains, above it all, calmly travelling outside the train coach. And, for a final time, I have recourse to the vision of the artist: a picture of Northrop Frye painted some fifteen years ago by Doug Martin with Frye brilliantly depicted above the mountains, as if suspended by an invisible chair in the heavens. Indeed, one does need 'improved binoculars' to see him.

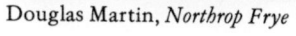

Douglas Martin, *Northrop Frye*

7

The End

Professor Frye gave the first University lecture that I ever attended. It ended with a reference to cultivating one's garden, and, indeed, the image of Voltaire's world has never been far from my mind in reading his texts. Needless to say, he is not responsible, nor any of the other teachers I have had, for the current state of my own garden. There have, nevertheless, been a number of people who have kindly helped with this study. The editors, Arthur Kroker and Marilouise Kroker, are largely responsible for the study being written. I thank them and the readers of the manuscript. I also thank Helen Ntoukas for her help with the word processing. Finally, I dedicate the study to Sheila, Andrew and D'Arcy.

Notes

Preface

1. Northrop Frye, *Divisions on a Ground,* Toronto: Anansi, 1982, p. 77.

1

1. N. Frye, *Fearful Symmetry,* Princeton: Princeton University Press, 1947, p. 340.
2. Terry Eagleton, *Literary Theory,* Minneapolis: University of Minnesota Press, 1983, p. 204.
3. See C.B. Macpherson, *The Political Theory of Possessive Individualism,* Oxford: Oxford University Press, 1962.

2

1. N. Frye, *The Great Code,* Toronto: Academic Press, 1981, p. 76.
2. N. Frye, *Fearful Symmetry,* preface.
3. *Ibid.,* p. 209.
4. E.J. Pratt, *Selected Poems,* Toronto: Macmillan, 1968, p. 185.
5. Samuel Beckett, *Endgame,* New York: Grove Press, 1958, p. 52.
6. William Blake, *Complete Writings,* Oxford: Oxford University Press, p. 149.
7. N. Frye, *Fearful Symmetry,* p. 49.
8. *Ibid.,* p. 159.
9. N. Frye, *The Return of Eden,* Toronto: University of Toronto Press, 1963, p. 21.
10. *Ibid.,* pp. 68-69.
11. *Ibid.,* p. 50.
12. *Ibid.,* p. 35.
13. N. Frye, *The Great Code,* p. 17.
14. *Ibid.,* pp. 17-18.
15. Robert Denham, *Northrop Frye's Critical Method,* University Park: Penn State University Press, 1978. Denham remarks on the difficulty of separating Frye from the authors he comments on. Denham's concern for Frye's literary criticism leads him away from the social and political vision that Frye is articulating which is the concern here.
16. Geoffrey Hartmann, *Criticism in the Wilderness,* New Haven: Yale University Press, 1980, p. 70.

17. N. Frye, *The Great Code*, p. 5.

18. *Ibid.*, p. xviii.

19. *Ibid.*, p. 7.

20. Eric Havelock, *The Liberal Temper of Greek Politics,* London: Jonathan Cape, 1957. Havelock represents the strongest advocate of technology believing that the essence of technology is at the core of liberal theory.

21. N. Frye, *The Great Code*, pp. 7-8.

22. *Ibid.*, p. 21.

3

1. Jean Baudrillard provides an interesting extension of Marshall McLuhan's insights into media. His analysis of capitalism in *Pour une critique de l'economic politique du signe,* Paris: Gallimard, 1972 provides striking argument that power has passed to the control of signs. See as well his argument concerning the death of the social in *À l'ombre des majorités silencieuses,* Paris: Éditions Denoel/Gonthier, 1982.

2. Dennis Lee's work is important exactly to the extent that he takes modernity and the nihilism of modern society seriously. *Savage Fields,* Toronto: Anansi, 1977 in particular depicts a grim vision that is only relieved by Lee's poetry, however much the poetry recognizes the 'savage fields.'

3. William Blake, "Auguries of Innocence," *The Complete Writings,* p. 433.

4. N. Frye, *Fables of Identity,* New York: Harcourt, Brace, Jonovich, 1963, p. 165.

5. N. Frye, *The Great Code*, p. 13.

6. N. Frye, *Fables of Identity*, p. 151.

7. *Ibid.*, p. 151.

8. N. Frye, *The Great Code*, p. 22.

9. F. Goya, "Capricho," No. 43. See as well David Cook, "The Sleep of Reason...," *C.J.P.S.T.,* Vol. 6, No. 1-2, 1982.

10. N. Frye, *The Great Code*, p. 37.

11. *Ibid.*, p. 187.

12. N. Frye, *Fables of Identity*, pp. 152-153.

13. *Ibid.*, p.30.

14. See N. Frye, *Fearful Symmetry*, p. 21.

15. Antoine de Saint Exupéry, *The Little Prince,* New York: Harcourt, Brace and World, 1943. Exupery was more concerned with existential themes than Frye, but he shares with Frye and a writer such as Albert Camus a sense that there must remain a sense of innocence in the natural world. Partially this was a reaction against the guilt of religion and the destruction of war which established nihilism as the fundamental problem for these writers.

16. Michel Foucault, *Madness and Civilization,* New York: Vintage Books, 1973. While Frye's sense of madness may be similar to Foucault, he stands opposed to Foucault in his defense of literary criticism as a field. Frye fails to recognize that the bounded discipline is a site of power and not a scientific fact.

17. N. Frye, *Fables of Identity,* p. 160.

18. N. Frye, "Expanding Eyes," *Spirtus Mundi,* Bloomington: Indiana University Press, 1976, The phrase comes from Blake's *The Four Zoas.*

19. N. Frye, "David Milne: An Appreciation," *The Bush Garden,* Toronto: Anansi, 1971.

20. *Ibid.,* p. 204.

21. *Ibid.,* p. 206.

22. See N. Frye, "Across the River and Out of the Trees," *Divisions on a Ground.*

23. N. Frye, *The Bush Garden,* p. 200.

24. *Ibid.,* pp. 222-223.

25. N. Frye, "Lawren Harris: An Introduction," *The Bush Garden.*

26. *Ibid.,* pp. 211-212.

4

1. The translation of the Psalm is taken from Joseph Pieper's, *Leisure: The Basis of Culture,* New York: Mentor-Omega Books, p. 19.

2. Thomas Hobbes, *Leviathan,* edited by C.B. Macpherson, Harmondsworth: Penguin Books, 1968, p. 75.

3. C.B. Macpherson, *The Political Theory of Possessive Individualism,* Oxford: Oxford University Press, 1962.

4. C.B. Macpherson, *The Life and Times of Liberal Democracy,* Oxford: Oxford University Press, 1977.

5. N. Frye, *The Critical Path,* Bloomington: Indiana University Press, 1971, p. 163.

6. Oswald Spengler, *The Decline of the West,* New York: Modern Library, 1932, p. 24.

7. *Ibid.,* p. 16.

8. N. Frye, *The Modern Century,* 1967, p. 42.

9. Spengler, *op. cit.,* p. 60.

10. N. Frye, *The Great Code,* p. 128.

11. O. Spengler, *op. cit.,* p. 35.

12. N. Frye, *The Return of Eden,* p. 143.

13. Immanuel Kant, *On History,* Indianapolis: The Library of Liberal Arts, 1963, p. 23.

14. *Ibid.*, p. 69.

15. *Ibid.*, p. 74 fn.

16. N. Frye, *Fearful Symmetry*, p. 13.

17. Michael Weinstein, *The Wilderness and the City*, Amherst: University of Massachusetts Press, 1982.

18. N. Frye, *The Great Code*, p. 94.

19. N. Frye, *The Critical Path*, p. 91.

20. *Ibid.*, p. 117.

21. *Ibid.*, p. 44.

22. John Locke, *Two Treatises of Government*, New York: Mentor Books, 1965, p. 387.

23. N. Frye, *The Critical Path*, p. 77.

24. William Blake, *Complete Writings*, pp. 635-636.

25. N. Frye, *The Modern Century*, p. 35.

26. *Ibid.*, p. 89.

27. N. Frye, *Divisions on a Ground*, p. 135.

28. N. Frye, *The Modern Century*, pp. 102-103.

29. N. Frye, *The Critical Path*, p. 106.

30. N. Frye, *Divisions on a Ground*, p. 100.

5

1. William Blake, *Complete Writings*, p. 196.

2. N. Frye, *The Secular Scripture*, Boston: Harvard University Press, 1976, p. 61.

3. N. Frye, *The Bush Garden*, p. 220.

4. The 'taciturn beaver' is Frye's phrase capturing, as it does, his sense of the symbolic strength of Canada.

5. William Blake, *op. cit.*, p. 197.

6. N. Frye, "Varieties of Literary Utopias," *The Stubborn Structure*, London: Methuen, 1970.

7. N. Frye, *The Bush Garden*, p. 222.

8. N. Frye points out that to the clerics riding circuit in Canada mosquitoes are a form of the fall.

9. N. Frye, *The Bush Garden*, pp. 141-142.

10. N. Frye, *Divisions on a Groud*, p. 76.

11. Frye, *Ibid.*, p. 43.

12. Arthur Kroker, *Technology and the Canadian Mind,* Montreal: New World Perspectives, 1984 and New York: St Martin's Press, 1985.

13. N. Frye, *The Bush Garden,* p. 247.

14. *Ibid.,* p. 249.

15. *Ibid.,* p. 238-239.

16. N. Frye, *Divisions on a Ground,* pp. 82-83.

17. *Ibid.,* p. 82.

18. Frederick Philip Grove, *A Search for America,* Toronto: McClelland and Stewart, 1971, p. x.

19. *Ibid.,* p. 382.

20. *Ibid.,* p. 382 fn.

21. Frye calls Pratt's poem "The Truant" the 'greatest poem in Canadian literature' which foreshadows in the dispute between the " 'great Panjandrum,' a demon of the mathematical order of nature" and humanity or the tension between technology and humanism. See *The Bush Garden,* p. 173.

6

1. The title "Improved Binoculars" is taken from the chapter ending of Frye's *The Modern Century.*

2. *Ibid.,* pp. 122-123.

3. N. Frye, *The Educated Imagination,* pp. 67-68.

4. Tom Wolfe, *The Painted Word,* New York: Bantam Books, 1975, p. 113.

Key Readings

A complete list of Frye's major publications up to 1974 may be found in Robert Denham's *Northrop Frye: An Enumerative Bibliography,* Metuchen, N.J.: Scarecrow Press, 1975. For those encountering Frye for the first time, I recommend *The Educated Imagination* published by the C.B.C. in 1963. Other works of Frye that are important to his social and political thought are as follows:

> *The Critical Path: An Essay on the Social Context of Literary Criticism,* 1971.
> *The Modern Century,* 1967.
> *The Bush Garden: Essays on the Canadian Imagination,* 1971.
> *Divisions on a Ground: Essay on Canadian Culture,* 1982.

I would also recommend *The Great Code,* 1981; *Fearful Symmetry: A Study of William Blake,* 1947; *The Return of Eden,* 1965; and the collection *Fables of Identity: Studies in Poetic Mythology,* 1963.

Other works of related interest are given below.

C.B. Macpherson, *The Real World of Democracy,* Toronto: C.B.C., 1965.

George Grant, *Lament for a Nation,* Toronto/Montreal: McClelland and Stewart, 1965.

George Grant, *Technology and Empire,* Toronto: Anansi, 1969.

Frederick Philip Grove, *A Search for America,* Toronto: McClelland and Stewart, 1971.

The Bible

William Blake, *Selected Poetry and Prose of Blake*, edited by Northrop Frye, New York: Modern Library College Editions, 1953.

Michael Weinstein, *The Wilderness and the City,* Amherst: The University of Massachusetts Press, 1982.

Arthur Kroker, *Technology and the Canadian Mind,* Montreal: New World Perspectives, 1984, and New York: St. Martin's Press, 1985.

Michael Ondaatje, *The Collected Works of Billy the Kid,* Toronto: Anansi, 1970.

Patricia Godsell, *Enjoying Canadian Painting,* Toronto: General Publishing, 1976.

Thomas Hobbes, *The Leviathan,* edited by C.B. Macpherson, Harmondsworth: Penguin Books, 1968.

John Locke, *The Two Treatises of Government,* New York: Mentor Books, 1965.

E.J. Pratt, *Selected Poems,* Toronto: Macmillan, 1968.

Jean Lipman and Tom Armstrong, editors, *American Folk Painters of Three Centuries,* New York: The Hudson Hill's Press, Inc., 1980.

LIST OF FIGURES

Many of the titles of the chapters and the titles of the subsections have been taken from Frye's work or from William Blake's.

I wish to thank Douglas Martin, Alex Colville and Marion Wagschall for permission to use their works.